CAPTURING SUCCESS

by
Vicki Hidde

DIAMOND MEDIA PRESS CO.
1-304-460-1427
https://www.diamondmediapressco.com/

Copyright © **2023**

By **Vicki Hidde**

ISBN Paperback: 978-1-954368-73-6

Dedication

Bob, Leah, Maddie, Caroline, and Will

Acknowledgments

As I recall all of the encouragement, suggestions, and prodding from my family, clients, friends, employees, and colleagues in human resources, I realize they all deserve much credit. Perhaps Cynthia Harnett and Jack Williams offered the most encouragement because their suggestions on clarity, style, and grammatical details were needed and appreciated. I am grateful to my friends, employees, and family, who allowed me to interrupt their busy lives and talk through the editing process. Sincere appreciation is also given to Kristine Sexter who first put this idea in my mind and Tate Publishing who made it a reality.

Table of Contents

Preface

AS YOU READ THE FOLLOWING pages, you may see a parallel between the ecosystem and the job-hunting landscape. Every species in the ecosystem uses a slightly different approach to finding their dinner and shelter. But at the end of the day, finding dinner, having shelter, and taking care of your family are all that matter.

Today we hear a lot about ecosystems and the value of every species in the local, regional, and international ecological network. We have instant access to information about the intricacies of tigers and ants by using Google to obtain complex details, much like a job search where there are page upon page of opinions and research. The information is readily available about employers who are hiring. The information is there for everyone to see, but it takes the best hunters, like the tigers, and most diligent data miners, like the ants, to find the fissure in the system. Only the best and brightest are able to exploit the information. By being at the right place at the right time, opportunity may find you.

For every species, there is a method for collecting food. Just like there is a method for finding jobs depending on your industry, location, and profession. To provide blanket advice for all job seekers is like telling the tiger to hunt like an ant and the ant to pounce like a tiger. Imagine for a moment tigers lining up like ants to hunt their prey. It is outside our reality to imagine one ant pouncing on something more than a breadcrumb. That just does not make a lot of sense, does it?

There are tigers that intimidate with their roar and ability to hunt prey. The tiger is known for pouncing quickly and dining after the hunt. On the other hand, the ant is known for methodically achieving tasks. They find the fissure, making a trail for other ants to follow as they find food. Ants are diligent and bring home food to the queen for all to feast upon.

Because of the many multi-generations within the job search ecosystem, there is a need to train and develop talent. Whether it is succession planning, setting the pace for excellence, or making a positive impact on the business culture, finding a small crack to facilitate change may be elusive. However, as the next generation emerges and raises the bar, innovations are soon to follow, as are profits.

Successful candidates for employment use what they know about the industry, their contacts, and personal uniqueness to create a plan. Whether they are a tiger or an ant, the seed for success is in each candidates mind. Sometimes it takes a little time to germinate before you get to the point that will propel you forward.

You may need to find a new industry, sharpen your skills, move to a new city, change careers, or obtain more education. There is a vast job search ecosystem and, as one human resource director told me, there is a good job for everyone. Don't you agree that it is time for you find you next best opportunity?

Now, I want to introduce you to two ants and a couple of their sidekicks:

WILLIE

Willie is the ant that is willing to go the extra mile, do what it takes, contribute, and is wise. He wants to learn and is coachable. Willie could also be a she, who is diligent and committed to excellence.

DISSIE

Dissie has a distorted view of the job search. Dissie wants everything right now, sees no value in working hard, and his attitude stinks at times. Like Willie, Dissie could be a she. She could spew toxicity and pollute the job search process.

From time to time, you may see more than one ant in a caption—these are the sidekicks. Also, in a few of the sections, you will see the ants used as bullets when there is a change of thought or a point is being made.

Introduction

As I visit with professionals in transition, I have learned that many of my clients get tunnel vision along with a blurred perspective and a distorted viewpoint of the job search landscape. Here are a few of the job search dots that you need to connect: experience, education, online job search, interviewing, networking, and salary negotiation. You will find others that are required for you to be successful.

While I will touch on the common areas, you will not find an in-depth discussion in this book. You will, however, find proven principles, illustrated concepts, and perhaps the trigger for your thought process to connect the job search dots for your specific career. Many dots go unnoticed by the average job seeker such as job stability, attitude, time management, trust, confidence, communication, rapport building, and respect.

As I visit in person or by phone with my clients, it is my goal to broaden their perspective and open their eyes to opportunities facing them in a changing economy. If this book can achieve that, perhaps it too will open the door to opportunity while challenging qualified candidates to broaden their skills and stretch their capabilities.

These opinions are based upon my experience and the experiences of my clients. For many years, there has been conflicting information spewing from the career communication pipeline. Most of this information is valid from the perception of the specific career expert. There are numerous lenses to examine job search and its many nuances.

As you read these short chapters and my observations of the job-search landscape, please realize that opinions are like the nose—everyone has one. If you find it challenging to distinguish between a job and a career, you will see that I add to the confusion by using "finding a job" and "establishing a career" interchangeably. But finding any job to pay the bills is not the same as establishing a career path and developing skills. If you want any job, go to any retailer, fast food restaurant, medical facility, or other organization known for less-than-lengthy employee retention and you can get a job. You may even find a career path in such an organization. This book is designed to help you distinguish between just a job to pay the bills and a career opportunity. Frequently, the job that just pays the bills turns into the one that offers promotion and challenge. Perhaps you will find your life's calling after sharing a few minutes of your time reading *Capturing Success By Connecting the Job Search Dots* and pondering your next career move.

Thank you for sharing your time. May you find it challenging and thought provoking as you explore new career horizons.

VICKI HIDDE

vickihidde@resume-source.com

(800) 650-2122

Thirteen Frequently Asked Questions by Job Seekers in a Booming Economy

1. How do I get started building a career that will offer a lifetime of promotion and career growth?

First, pinpoint the type of people who challenge you to perform outside your comfort zone. Surround yourself with people who demand your best. Identify the skills you want to use, along with your strengths and weaknesses. Ask yourself, "What skills can I develop that will accelerate my career, stretch my capabilities, and raise the bar on my true potential?" *I am sure you will agree that this tidbit will work in any economy.* Before you move on, spend time contemplating the two following questions:

- Have you developed a mental performance ceiling for your career growth?

- Who are the people who can and will help you get ahead?

Rarely do I write a résumé for a watchmaker. In fact, I can count on one hand the number of résumés I have written for these highly skilled specialists. I did not realize that Oklahoma State University in Okmulgee offers such a program. That is, until a student graduating at the top of his class contacted me to build his résumé. He wanted a job with a leading Swiss watchmaker. This client had a master's degree in a social science and a successful career—he was unfulfilled and wanted more. He said the company that interested him the most never hired recent graduates. He asked my advice and we prepared what most in the résumé writing arena would consider an over-the-top presentation. He landed an interview. Then he was offered a position with the Swiss watchmaker in New York. While I would like to take credit for his success, the offer had more to do with his drive for excellence than the résumé. Or did it?

If you are launching a career upon graduation as a traditional student, you will find that academic success is highly valued by most if not all major corporations. Many employers are looking for students who graduated in the top 10 percent of their class. Other companies are looking for strengths in specific areas. Employers are impressed when you do your homework and can tell them about their company.

You will find many examples with an Oklahoma launch point for careers as you read this book. In fact, I cannot think of a state where I have either written a résumé for a candidate or had a client targeting an opportunity in other states. Many of clients find lucrative positions in major metropolitan area. I have written résumés for recent graduates who were targeting positions in New York City, Chicago, Florida, California and most other states. They had big dreams. In some cases, I was surprised when those dreams became a reality. Other times, I expected their success.

One recent graduate told me, "I want to work for the number one ad agency in New York". She was happy when she landed a job with the number two agency in New York City.

Another client moving to Chicago shared with me that the hiring manager said, "You had the best résumé in our candidate pool." As she changes jobs, I still work with her on developing a résumé that pinpoints her most marketable skills.

Still another called from the Middle East and needed a résumé for a new contract position. In fact this has happened several times.

On another occasion, I was writing résumés for an executive and the administrative team for a global company with their headquarters in St. Louis. The company had a facility in Korea and the plant manager needed a résumé to find another global position. He had a short timeline and we were able to create a résumé that pinpointed his skills so he could move his career forward.

As veterans return from their military service, they need more than a résumé that explains their skills and experience. They need a résumé to show their discipline, work ethic and drive.

When you are reinventing yourself and making a career change, you will need to identify your transferable skills. Then match those skills with the requirements of the organization, which can benefit from your experience.

WILLIE

Take the pulse of the job market in your area or where you want to live! Identify the reality of the job market as you begin to connect your dots for success.

Many of the best jobs are with your current employer. Dave Blankenship, who retired as Corporate Vice President of External Affairs from Rockwell International, said he always wanted to know why a candidate did not take the steps necessary to develop talent for his or her current employer. He wanted to see employee progression. He expected employees to take advantage of opportunities for cross training and dedication to corporate goals. Mr. Blankenship also indicated that military promotions and training played a pivotal role in hiring or promotion decisions.

WILLIE 
Why not explore internal career options before you plan a drastic career change.

2. WHEN IS A GOOD TIME TO THINK ABOUT A JOB SEARCH?

While not losing focus on how important it is to spend your new employee capital wisely, you can make a good case for thinking about future steps in your career before beginning your first day on the new job. Exercise caution when voicing your desire to move too rapidly through the ranks. After thirty days or so on the job, update your résumé with key responsibilities, special projects, and accomplishments. Be prepared to navigate your career through each phase of the learning process.

 **DISSIE**

What is new employee capital?

Whether it's your first day on the job, six months into a new position or fifteen years down the road, why not list career options and ponder any career moves you see on your individual career landscape. Do this on a regular basis before you need your next job. You may want to carve out some time by making an appointment with yourself to evaluate potential career options.

A corporate attorney who led the intellectual property legal team for an emerging technology company remarked, "I want to stay ahead of the curve and be prepared before I need a new position. I could need a job soon…"

 **DISSIE**

Is reading tea leaves a talent?

WILLIE 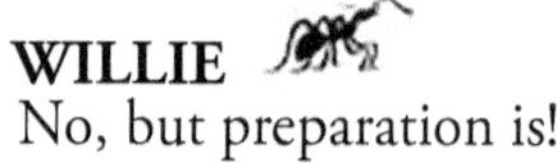
No, but preparation is!

3. WHERE ARE THE JOBS IN TODAY'S ECONOMY?

Jobs are sensitive to politics, new technology, economic cycles, environmental regulations, changes in the management team, the financial health of companies, and more. By regularly reading online industry-specific journals and print publications, you can keep abreast of industry trends and identify potential employment opportunities. Looking for jobs with leading edge companies is like catching a wave—you want the thrill of riding the top of the wave without being caught in the undercurrent of lost opportunity.

Each industry has economic indicators. One that leaps to mind is fuel. Perhaps I am sensitive to job gains and job losses due to fuel cost because of the regional employment base. While areas of the Colorado, Washington, Georgia, Oklahoma, Kansas, Florida and Texas economies are diversified, there are many world-class energy and aerospace companies located in pockets throughout the region and country. Fuel cost is an economic driver with far-reaching economic impact.

American Airlines is a large employer, which impacts a wide array of regional, national and international businesses. Other touch-points include the energy, transportation, and manufacturing sectors. When jet fuel costs are escalating, the aviation industry experiences losses—diesel cost pushes transportation expenses out of sight and this price tag is a touch-point for everything we purchase. Fuel outlay impacts utilities and consumers feel the pinch, as do many industries. Sadly, job loss follows. There are other commodities, political situations, and cost of money fluctuations, which can bring any economy to its knees. When the financial industry experiences a meltdown, it impacts global markets.

At this writing, American Airlines has filed for bankruptcy; jobs, pensions and healthcare benefits are in jeopardy. While the jobs have not evaporated yet, there is a potential for job loss. A suitor may appear on the horizon to save the day for the employees, but there are not many options available to the AA management team.

One of my clients told me that tractor trucks would be parked on the side of the road when fuel hit a certain dollar mark. When that happened, trucking firms collapsed and there were trucks sitting at terminals and truck stops across the nation.

A few years ago, a tax was levied on yachts and the industry suffered. People who could afford a "big boat" looked internationally to make such purchases.

The publishing industry is not immune to technology changes and industry pressures. When I began putting my notes on strips of paper and writing this book, professionals read books. Today, many of those same professionals are getting most of their information from blogs, the internet or eBooks. The publishing industry is experiencing many shifts and there is job loss or repurposing of tasks.

If you are a small business, it may be difficult to find funding sources, due to the new controls placed on banks and financial institutions.

During the economic cycle of 2008-2012, nationally, we experienced job losses in the automobile, financial, and manufacturing sectors. Many locations are and have experienced double-digit unemployment. You could say it had a domino effect on other industries. Government cut backs have affected aerospace engineers at NASA in Texas, Alabama and Florida. Many economists are predicting that the current downturn could be with us for two to five years.

Innovation, environmental impact, and regulation challenges influence companies as well. Even changes in the tax code can cause industry decline and job loss.

WILLIE 
The fallout of change results in both job loss and
hiring opportunities.

Agriculture industry leaders have transformed the agricultural chemical industry by creating a chemistry and seed technology that influences agricultural chemical sales—leaving competition scrambling for competitive solutions. When patents expire, leaders move quickly to introduce pace-setting innovations to maintain the competitive advantages. This model plays out in many industries.

Other manufacturers developed closed-loop systems to eliminate environmental impact and costly permitting processes. One company manufactures shingles for residential roofs in an industry plagued with environmental issues. The closed-loop system and engineering design improved processes and reduced startup cost while surpassing environmental compliance requirements.

WILLIE
With each innovation, the next waves of technical jobs are born.

Innovation along with environmental impact continually change—job creation finds its level—just like water during a flood.

The examples listed above may have nothing to do with your specific job search. However, raw material costs, energy expenses, innovation, vanishing technologies, labor shortages, cost of money, and environmental impact can and does influence job markets. Another factor that influences job creation is emerging technologies.

New Job Creation

Early in my management career, I was having a discussion with a successful engineer. He said, "Read any advertisement for a technical position and 50 percent of new job creation is in industries that did not exist five years ago." Today, new job creation is measured in months rather than years. Whether it is the next generation of Facebook, a Google innovation, Smart Phone Application or Medical breakthrough, there are new jobs that go unfilled in any economy. Frequently, I tell my clients, "Read newspapers from major cities where innovation is fertile, read trade journals and conduct online research in key metropolitan areas and see what jobs are hot and go unfilled." I would shout this from the roof top if I thought folks would listen. Recently, I heard a speaker say that 70 percent of the population has poor listening habits. To be direct, that is probably both you and me.

If you are a CD manufacturer, that technology is being replaced with the "Cloud" and other devices such as flash drives. Technology shifts require us to add to our skill-toolbox and carry the attitude of, yes I want to learn. In today's economy, nothing replaces an inquisitive nature and the desire to learn.

You may need retraining and have five jobs in the next five years as the economy responds to these technology shifts.

It is a fact that by the time that certain devices are introduced into the market, that technology is obsolete. Each year, I purchase at least one computer and either love or hate the improvements. Change and learning are here to stay. You can get ahead of the curve by not waiting until tomorrow to get started. Take action today!

Bonus

I asked this same professional, who opened my eyes to technical job growth, "How do you hire good people?" His advice has served me well throughout my career when making hiring decisions. He said, "Identify three qualifying questions for each position. Those three questions will lead to deeper discussions during the interview process." His simple approach is invaluable. In my hiring, I found that I could develop talent, if the candidate had the "want to" and two of the talents the questions uncovered. I could teach the third. But, if I could get all three, the client could hit the ground running. If they had only one of the requirements, they failed. With this approach, I was able to improve employee retention and achieve ambitious performance benchmarks.

Today, candidates are being interviewed using automation to record answers to questions that qualify candidates.

The questions are designed to determine a candidate's understanding of the specific job requirements. Assessment tests are given to determine the best candidates. Content experts are in short supply across multiple disciplines.

 **DISSIE**
Employers want the *best* candidate. Will ranking in the top 75 percent get me the job?

WILLIE 
If you plan to excel, perform in the top 10 percent.

Knowing When It Is Time to Move on

Throughout my career, I have attended numerous seminars where the speakers talked about human capital, employee retention, succession planning, and employee relations. Executives are frequently quoted as saying that good employees don't leave the company. They leave bad bosses. After interviewing thousands of professionals in transitions, this is true.

One such client in a niche financial sales arena had been with the company for twentythree years and had a continual career progression. I would rank him in the top 5 percent of his field.

"You must have a stinker for a boss," I said without thinking.

A poker face stared back at me. Unfortunately, I thought that I had overstepped and intruded into an area that was inappropriate. At our next meeting, he said, "The last time we met you described my boss without meeting him. I am amazed with your insight."

 **DISSIE**

Are you upset yet? I think people work better when I nag them. What can I say to needle you?

WILLIE

All I want to do is take care of my customers and make a profit—I wish you would be more supportive.

Over the course of one week, I had one person tell me I was a psychic and another tell me I was a prophet. I am neither. It is Human Behavior 101. Job openings are created by both good bosses and bad ones alike. Good bosses keep expanding their responsibilities and employee base while bad bosses have a revolving door in their departments and find it necessary to replace good employees. Good bosses have the ability to challenge their team to excel and exceed goals.

If you take a survey of the talents of good bosses, you will find them to be consistent, intolerant of drama in the workplace, and encourage their subordinates to stretch their capabilities. They keep their team focused on the project or task at hand. Not only are they good listeners, but they require their team to come up with their own solutions, while encouraging individuals to take the initiative.

Bad bosses belittle their staff, take on an air of superiority and are quick to remind everyone they are the boss and know best. They encourage drama in the workplace by showing partiality, double dealing and distracting the team. You can see the inconsistencies in the way they handle projects, assign tasks and allocate resources. They hold the future of their staff in their hands and they like to hold that power over the employees' heads. They will brag about their process working, when everyone but them knows it is a flop.

One of my employees gave me the "Bad Boss B's". She was telling me about a boss from a former career. Her list included backstabbing, badgering, belittling, blaming and babbling. I hope I don't fall into any of these areas as a leader.

This same employee said that she appreciates being invited into the decision making process and welcomes praise and encouragement. Don't we all?

These bad bosses force their employees to choose between their values and their job.

When a boss is tempted to micromanage, rethinking, not over-thinking, the decision is always appropriate. While it is important to hold your staff accountable, micromanaging can demoralize the best employee. Clear and direct expectations are essential to measuring performance.

The One Minute Manager by Ken Blanchard is an excellent book for managers. I need to reread it at least annually to keep focused. It is a short read for any supervisor.

Good managers challenge their teams to set high goals and surpass expectations.

Good bosses will develop a plan and execute with precision. They will involve the team in order to get a personal buy-in from each team member.

One way to learn more about a company is to accept a *temporary assignment* or contract position through an agency. You will be able to obtain firsthand knowledge regarding the corporate culture and work environment before you make a commitment. This is an excellent method for researching new career opportunities.

Many times, the only way to get your foot into the door of a major company is to accept a temporary assignment. Major companies have contracts with national and international employment agencies to fill vacancies. These positions may or may not be permanent ones. If you are a top performer you may transform a temporary assignment or special project into a permanent position.

Technical professionals with specialized expertise earn top dollar for their skill set. The downside to this arrangement is that the contractors must provide their own benefits and health insurance. When the project goes away, so does the job. Usually there is another one around the corner.

Unfortunately, many unemployed candidates have had a bad experience with a temporary agency. Sometimes, it is the worst bosses and unproductive companies who need a staff for a special project. Asking your friends for a referral to a temporary company is one of the best ways to hook up with a good agency.

Many times, there are jobs working for the agency as a recruiter, human resource generalist or onsite supervisor. If you accept a business development position you will have the opportunity to market the agency's services and make contacts with business leaders. This could put you in a position to be recruited away from the agency into a more lucrative role.

DISSIE

Working temporary would be great! Maybe I could work six hours each day, for three days a week—could I get a full-time paycheck?

What industries interest you?

____

____

____

What job titles interest you?

____

____

Recap

Your individual approach to the job opportunities may be like collecting low-hanging fruit. Or it could require exploration of obscure, hard-to-find places.

DISSIE

Are we picking peaches or looking for a job?

Any personal plan requires the ability to analyze the local job market, industry trends, and financial health of an organization, along with your ability to perform. Many times, by listening and observing, plus some legwork and research, you can uncover job opportunities where seemingly none exists. When looking for a better job, make sure you find a strong management team—one that will provide prolific opportunity so you can stretch your skills and reach new career heights.

One executive that I know hired a craftsman who had written his résumé on a white paper plate. It worked. I have heard stories of people getting hired off of a cocktail napkin and brown paper bag. When the job market is strong and top talent is in short supply, managers recruit at restaurants, when purchasing a new wardrobe, or on a hunting trip. It could be on the golf course or ski trip that an opportunity presents itself.

4. WHAT ABOUT POSTING RÉSUMÉS ONLINE?

Another of the many dots is online job search and its effectiveness. For decades, finding the "right" job was more about relationships than about sending résumés or posting them online. The caveat is, if you possess technical knowledge or specialized expertise that is in short supply, you'll find web-based searches advantageous.

After interviewing human resource professionals, I learned that certain questions are placed in the online application as screening tools to push people out of the selection process. In other words, if a question is answered one way, you get to move to the next step; if it is answered another, you are kicked out of the system and eliminated from consideration.

 **DISSIE**
I have completed hundreds of online applications.
Am I answering the questions wrong?

In a recent discussion with a fifty-plus-yearold professional, he said, "In years past, scam jobs were published in the newspaper. Now those same folks or their cousins have moved to the Internet. Apply for jobs today and you will have network marketing and 'have I got a deal for you' bottom feeders contacting you about straight-commission or 'send me $25.00 to $300.00' and I'll set you up in business opportunities."

WILLIE
These folks are working very hard to convince me
this is a wonderful opportunity, don't you think?

During a question-and-answer session at a local university, one participant said, "I have a solution to minimize calls from the Internet."

"What is your solution?" I asked.

"In my correspondence, I asked to be contacted for positions in my field that offers a salary in excess of $65K. My calls are now limited to serious employers."

Knowing salary discussion can be tricky, especially before a mutual interest is established, you need to carefully consider divulging salary requirements. Is it worth the risk to discuss salary in early stages of the job search? In tough economic times, it could be dicey, but during a labor shortage there is room for debate. I lean toward discussing salary after you know more about the job.

WILLIE 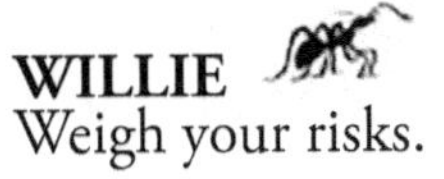
Weigh your risks.

Which websites have you visited?

____

____

____

Are you using LinkedIn, Plaxo, Facebook, etc.?

____

____

Caution

With the prevalence of identity theft, one internet security expert recommends that you *set up a job-search e-mail address,* use no personal information on your document and be selective with who sees your confidential information. *Remember to check this e-mail regularly.*

Confidential information includes social security number or other sensitive information. Many recruiters will block your current employer's names. Some companies use data mining to uncover employees who are searching for a new job. If your identity has been stolen or your credit damaged by the misfortune, it could disqualify you as a candidate for the perfect job. While it is not your fault, it is messy.

5. What are the tools I need to begin an effective job search?

For years, résumés and cover letters would open doors for you. Now the situation is thorny. With the onset of Twitter®, LinkedIn®, Monster®, Career Builder®, Hot Jobs®, search engines, company websites, and other job search sites, we have job search advice at our fingertips. It can take hours to complete multiple applications with a host of companies.

Everyone needs an up-to-date résumé. Everyone! As an employee, you never know when you will be tapped for a promotion and have your superior request a copy of your résumé—one thrown together at midnight may diminish your credibility. Then there is an interview process, where the résumé can provide a roadmap for the discussion.

A competitor may contact you with an opportunity that could double your salary. Listening to an offer can be in your best interest. I would recommend that you always listen to new opportunities. Always!

Well-written résumés are more important than ever in today's job market. Some companies expect cover letters while others do not. Our research indicates that 60 percent of our clients achieved better results with a cover letter. Sometimes, the recruiter views the cover letter as just disjointed characters and more online pollution that clogs the job search pipeline.

When I see an uncovered, naked résumé without a cover letter, I always ask myself, "What do I need to do with this?" It usually makes it to the circular file quickly or I use the delete key.

DISSIE

Did I hear someone say something about going naked to do your job hunting?

From time to time, I advertise for a writer. About 50 percent of the time, there is no cover letter attached. By attaching a cover letter you show the reader that you can write, persuade and explain your point of view. It is true that some companies and recruiters do not require a cover letter. However, organizations that require writing skills want to see how you construct a sentence. I have read letters where the writer uses humor, sarcasm and from time to time they provide unnecessary minutia. It is important to set a tone of competence, if you expect to land the interview. This point is illustrated below.

A sales executive told one of my clients, "You're really not qualified, but after reading your cover letter, I wanted to meet you to determine if you would be a good match for our company." She did not fit their criteria, but she landed the interview and obtained good interviewing experience. She also made a good contact.

One of my clients, who had been asked to resign because he would not doctor the accounts receivable records, was dismissed. I prepared a letter stating that he ensured the integrity of financial records and he landed the job within days after losing his job.

Two other tools are needed. One is a phone and the other is a computer. Record a professional voice-mail and use a professional e-mail address. Your professional voice mail message and email address speaks not only to your competence, but your understanding of business. Your friends may understand your humor or sarcasm, but the future employer may be less than impressed.

"This is Vicki Hidde. Thank you for calling. I'll be in touch soon."

Instead of perfectwriter@resume-source.com, try Vicki@resume-source.com.

In today's job market, you need a presence on LinkedIn, along with a profile. When you are actively asking questions and participating in discussions, you earn the respect of your peers. If you are on Facebook, before you upload your photo album with an adult beverage in your hand, you might want to rethink that decision. If there is a controversial area of your life, whether politics, religion, or lifestyle, some things need to remain private. There is a real world out there. Being authentic is important, but you don't need to reveal too much information. Keep it professional. Whether you are using social media, telephone contact, or a one-on-one discussion, it cannot be all about you. Try listening more than you talk.

6. How can I research the company's salary range and benefits?

Everyone wants to know the salary range of the position. Salary negotiation is another of the job search dots. Many companies explain their benefits in recruitment material or the information is available online at the company website. Some companies are private and this information is guarded.

If you know someone who works for the company that you are targeting, you can ask questions regarding the salary range of positions with the company. There are differing opinions on approaching salary discussions. Some feel that by asking this question early in the process, you can avoid wasting time.

My opinion is that you must build value before you begin the negotiation phase. Never be the first to bring up salary and benefits during the interview process. *Never! Never! Never!* You may want to try the following response to, "What salary do you expect?"

"You're a fair company, and I am sure you will make a competitive offer—if I am the right candidate for your company. Do you mind sharing the salary range of the position?"

Many of the clients I work with believe that companies want to hammer employees for the lowest salary possible.

While this is sometimes true, salary is many times used as a yardstick for performance and responsibility level.

After we facilitated an outplacement assignment for a group of professionals, one of the candidates obtained an interview with a premier company. A few minutes into the interview, the candidate was asked, "How much money did you make last year?" He responded with a number lower than industry standard. The position paid twice what he was making. He was deemed unqualified by the interviewer and the discussion ended rather abruptly.

Human resource professionals frequently take salary surveys in order to determine the competitiveness of their offers. You may be asked for a salary history. You may need this tool in your job search.

Your salary history shows, in black and white, a clear income progression. Documented salary history can be used as a negotiation tool.

7. How do I become a good online researcher?

Search engines are wonderful. Practice improves your skill level. Large urban library systems subscribe to databases. Many resources can be accessed online with a library card. For other resources, you will need to take a trip to the library. These complex databases will provide demographic, statistical, economic, and financial information regarding targeted companies. Many libraries offer classes to walk you through the research process. The Tulsa City County Library offers "Ask the Librarian", a free service to Tulsa County residents. It also offers research service where you can pay for more complex information and reports. *Libraries and businesses throughout the country use Tulsa's Library Fee-based services. While this may appear to be unnecessary information that makes me look like I am regional in scope, I have traveled nationally and been able to obtain the required information from the Tulsa City County Library, when other major city libraries would not respond to my request.*

The point here is to know the resources available through your library system.

One of my clients was relocating to the Washington, DC area. She was a professional medical library manager, who told me that she didn't need my help researching job search databases. This was after I had printed my online findings. Then we both discovered that I had uncovered at least twenty job openings in my search that were not on her list. There is so much information and many times the jobs are disguised with vague job titles. Finding the ones that suit you best may be hidden in unlikely places with unique job titles.

Research the various job boards and see which companies are hiring. With a little research, you can find the information that your job search requires. Today there are hundreds of organizations maintaining job databases. The more common ones are listed below:

- Monster.com
- Hotjobs.com
- Careerbuilder.com
- Dice.com
- Flipdog.com
- Nationjob.com
- USAJOBS.com
- Craigslist.com
- TweetMyJobs.com

8. How do I effectively prepare for the interview?

Whether you are applying for a job in Tulsa, New York City, Seattle, Los Angeles, Phoenix, Minneapolis, Las Vegas or a Denver based company, or in Europe, Asia and the Middle East, interviewing is all about preparation. Many folks think they can wing it and land the job. Perhaps they can. Don't you want more than just a job that pays the bills? With proper preparation, you may create a job for yourself that will position you for a lifetime of promotion.

First, look at your background and identify ten questions that you anticipate the potential employer will ask. In addition, you want to do this before you send the first résumé. *You will find more information on this in chapter six.*

9. How do i build a contact base of influential business leaders and leverage their experience to push my career forward?

Networking, connecting with thought leaders, and finding a good mentor can be a challenge. There are questions that you must answer before you approach someone you want to mentor you.
Why should the mentor invest his or her time in you?

____

____

____

What are the benefits of taking you on as a project?

____

____

____

Do you have the work ethic to become a next-generation leader?

Once you have more than self-serving answers to the above questions, develop a list of ten acquaintances, either who can serve as a mentor or who knows someone that will. Why not approach two or three of your contacts to schedule an informational interview? Make an honest assessment of the interviews and then refine your approach before you contact three more. Repeat the process until you find a mentor. You may want to contact your colleagues in your cell phone directory, Outlook, or use LinkedIn. Make a few contacts and be interested in the person you are calling.

Bonus

When networking with your peers, remember you are competing for the same positions. Your peers may be reluctant to share contact information in fear of losing the career race. Build a network at least one level up.

One of My Mentoring Experiences

Early in my career, I hired and mentored Ed. He was bright, creative, and challenging to supervise. His mother was a single mom with three children. Upon graduation from high school, he got angry with his mom and me and joined the Marine Corps. We lost touch for twenty-plus years. Then I got a call and he wanted to do lunch. I had a previous engagement, so he stopped by my office after lunch.

"I went to the University of Tulsa before lunch and picked up a copy of my Bachelor of Electrical Engineering degree. I took a job with the federal government, started immediately and did not pick up my degree. After all the tales I told you over the years, I knew you would never believe that I completed a degree if you did not see the copy. Vicki, I would never have completed the degree if it weren't for you. You helped me find success. Thank you."

Everyone is busy and as we slowly walk through the business crowd, it is important that leaders leave the business world better than we found it and by mentoring we can do so.

WILLIE
If given the opportunity, become a mentor.

10. How can I find the core competency requirements of employers?

This is where you can let your fingers and knowledge of research work for you. Let the Internet help you research the company's mission, values, and successes. You can research the biographies of executives who work for the company, find articles they have written, and listen to local and national interviews of corporate leaders. Investor Relations sections of company websites will give you a window into the company's vision. Additionally, you can research job positions to see what qualities the company values. Is what the company portrays through their mission and values consistent with your research?

Occasionally, I will do a search for specific job skills in Seattle, Chicago, Atlanta, Houston, etc. The purpose of the search is to get a feel for the language required for specific job descriptions. I know full well the language may not be effective in my region of the country. This exercise allows me to get a window into the intricacies of specific jobs.

As part of your research, you may need to evaluate the positions one level up from your skills set as well as one level below. This information could become vital as you continue your job search.

11. Do i need a degree, license, or certification to...?

I am sure you will agree that we want neuro surgeons educated and licensed. Education is valuable in today's business environment. A bachelor's degree is the minimum requirement for many positions. Today, companies are asking for an MBA before the candidate can enter a corporate management-training program. These companies are looking for talent, knowledge of current business practices, critical thinking skills, and a strategic approach to integrating business solutions.

One day, a gentleman walked in and the first words to fall from his lips were, "My friends say that I have a bad attitude. What do you think?"

"Let's talk about that in just a minute."

As the story unfolded, I discovered that he completed truck-driving school and accepted an apprenticeship-like trucking driving position, which took nine weeks to complete. Two weeks before receiving the CDL endorsement, he decided to quit the program and return home. Then he could not understand why no one would hire him.

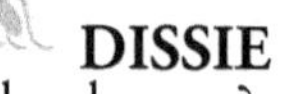 **DISSIE**

So you think that I have a bad attitude, do you?

Companies are looking for resilient employees who can overcome adversity while maintaining a positive attitude.

12. How do i take my career to the next level?

Education is foundational and one of the dots that must be connected as you seek new career opportunities. If you need an advanced degree to push your career forward, then it is up to you to make it happen. Education alone doesn't always propel you to the next level. You will find that a combination of education, can-doattitude, discipline, effective communication skills, and the ability to quickly build rapport will pave the way for the next step in your career progression.

WILLIE
Education, certification, and licensing are not an entitlement to *success*—just a ticket to get you into the game.

A few years ago, I was visiting with a community college administrator and she said, "Many of our students hold a bachelor's degree, but they see the need to expand their technical knowledge and they are completing coursework to obtain new skills. Today's work force is an educated and highly skilled one."

When you develop your annual career plan, integrate educational enrichment through independent reading or college courses. If you want to kill your career, do nothing.

Another way to sharpen your skills is to become active in professional organizations, where you can collaborate with key industry leaders.

I was having a discussion with a vice president of marketing and she said, "I spent years getting my degrees and obtaining my experience. When I have a business problem now, I contact a peer who I trust and I seek out his or her advice. This is how I learn today."

On another occasion, I was visiting with a real estate professional who said, "I have a few brokers throughout the country who are leaders in their markets and we collaborate at least once each year. I am amazed at how these talks challenge each of us." Have you asked your supervisor what it would take to develop the talent to move your career up the corporate ladder?

13. When I get an offer, how do I manage the process?

If you're working with a recruiter, take your lead from the recruiter and follow directions carefully. Recruiters know their client and they understand the process. In most cases, the recruiter negotiates your salary. This is not the time to throw the recruiter a curve. Make sure all your questions are answered before you get to this point. Recruiters work for the company and they have the tasks of locating the "best" candidate available for the position.

Recruiters know their client's corporate culture and it is vital that you be honest with the recruiter—let them coach you through the process. In the total job search scheme of things, recruiters place about 5 percent of candidates into new jobs.

WILLIE

If you don't have a recruiter, you need a plan.

An MBA client was interviewing with a small headquarter company with five or six executives. They needed a vice president of marketing. She and her husband discussed the salary range and she settled on a number. At the meeting where she was offered the job, they offered her $15,000 more than she expected. Everything in her wanted to jump up and say "Yes! Yes!" She felt it prudent to say, "I'll get back with you." At the next meeting, she told the executives she could accept the position if they added $15,000 more to the initial offer. They agreed to her request.

WILLIE
Some employers and department heads expect you to negotiate.

There was an engineer with a recently earned master's degree, who was offered a position at $12,000 under what she expected. She told the aviation company that she would get back with them. After about three weeks, the recruiter called back and offered her $17,000 more and she took the job.

WILLIE
Patience works well as a negotiation tool.

THIRTEEN FREQUENTLY ASKED QUESTIONS BY JOB SEEKERS IN A BOOMING ECONOMY

1. How do I get started building a career that will offer a lifetime of promotion and career growth?

2. When is a good time to think about a job search?

3. Where are the jobs in today's economy?

4. Should I post my résumé online?

5. What are the tools I need to begin an effective job search?

6. How can I research the company's salary range and benefits?

7. How do I become a good online researcher?

8. How do I effectively prepare for the interview?

9. How do I build a contact base of influential business leaders and leverage their experience to push my career forward?

10. How can I find the core competency requirements of employers?

11. Do I need a degree, license or certification to...?

12. How do I take my career to the next level?

13. When I get an offer, how do I manage the process?

Twelve Frequently Asked Questions by Job Seekers in a Weak Economy

1 . How can I support myself in a bad economy?

In the initial stage of a downward economic cycle, I had a conversation with one of my clients with an MBA who had a successful career in the telecommunications industry. The company was moving his area to the east coast and he wanted to live elsewhere.

Knowing that innovation finds fertile ground during economic downturns, I commented, "You and four or five of your buddies are going to be playing golf, sipping on adult beverages, or spending a weekend at the lake. One of you will say, I have this idea for…then you will create a business plan. Three years down the road, you will have built a $10 million business."

WILLIE
There are times in your career when you look at the economic landscape, define opportunity, and make things happen.

41

For others experiencing the sting of recession, it will require that you take a second or possibly third job to support your family. It is not the end of the world when this happens. During this whirlwind, you may discover what you want out of your work life and have the drive to make it happen.

WILLIE 

While I'm a good ant—fire ants are vicious like a recession. They pack a mighty sting.

In the summer of 2009, I met a young man who had just completed two MBA degrees and was ready to launch his career. I found it interesting how he supported his lifestyle in college. He created a business plan, secured a $20,000 loan, and opened a summer business. No doubt he has the Midas touch, because he paid off that loan in five and a half weeks and went on to open four more shops.

A lady who is known for her culinary skills needed extra Christmas cash. Her friends were busy with holiday entertaining and purchased goodies from her. She made the extra cash by baking holiday treats and they served delicious treats.

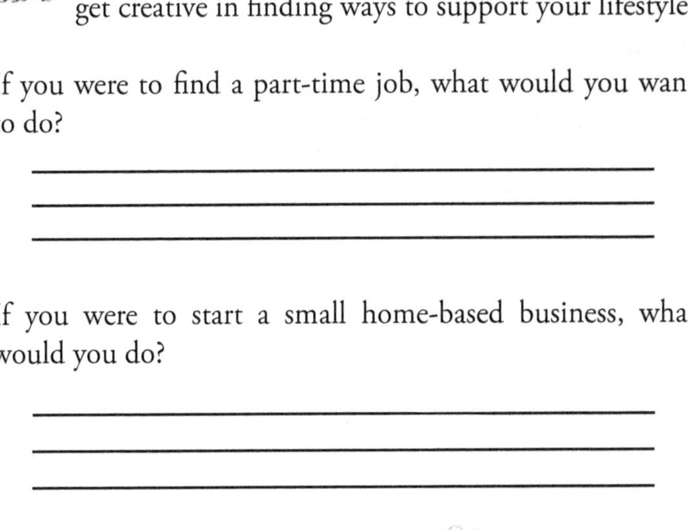

During an economic downturn, you may need to get creative in finding ways to support your lifestyle.

If you were to find a part-time job, what would you want to do?

____

____

____

If you were to start a small home-based business, what would you do?

____

____

____

DISSIE

There has to be a better job than working in the ant farm.

2. WHAT ARE MY MOST MARKETABLE SKILLS?

How long has it been since you listed your skills? Most of us do not see clearly the things that we do well. Even fewer of us can identify our transferable skills. If you find yourself in this dilemma, ask friends to help you identify your most marketable skills. Prioritize your list by cataloging the skills you like to use most. Also, make a list of things you do not like to do. Then focus on jobs that require the talents you like to use. If you need more training to validate or certify those skills, consider enrolling in a program with that goal in mind. It could be the best investment of your life.

 **DISSIE**

But I only know how to be an ant.

List your transferable skills here:

____

____

____

Just listing that you are a people-person and like to have fun is not enough. There is strategy in listing transferrable skills to make the most impact.

3. Who is hiring in times like these?

Now this is where you have to use brainstorming skills. Recently, I visited a couple of retail stores at a local mall, and as I walked the mall, I saw several signs saying, "We're hiring." One of my clients said, "I'll take anything." When I shared this information with her I heard, "But I don't want to work evenings…I don't want to work weekends." Therefore, she was saying, "I have certain expectations from the job." There is nothing wrong with outlining your criteria for the next step in your career.

What type of jobs appeal to you?

____

____

____

By identifying industrial parks, Class A office complexes and medical institutions, you will have opportunity to research companies in these areas. You can use the same observation skills to see if you're targeting companies that are hiring.

There have been *three memorable* times when I have made recommendations and my potential clients looked back at me with penetrating eyes of disbelief. The following is one such story. Some years ago, I was in a city where the unemployment rate was 14.9 percent. That city was Shreveport, Louisiana. As I coached job seekers, I told them companies were hesitant to post an ad if they were looking for a few good people. The company would be inundated with thousands of résumés and phone calls, because people were desperate. Their overworked staff was already stretched and such an announcement would cause an avalanche of paper. Today, their inbox would overflow. Companies can receive one thousand résumés for one opening. Over half of the candidates do not meet the minimal requirements.

When my clients contacted companies directly, many times they found openings. They would tell me, "What you said worked great. I went to work for 'ABC Company.'"

Admittedly, this was before the Internet, but this advice still works today with a twist. Now you must jump through the Internet hoops which human resources uses to protect their time, streamline the application process, and ensure regulatory compliance. If you can find the name of the hiring authority and submit your résumé, you may find an open position where none existed until your résumé crossed the desk of the manager—because only the department manager can identify underperformers. Then the manager can communicate with HR, asking them to schedule an interview with the potential candidate and begin the selection process.

DISSIE
Now, it is time to think outside of the box! Is that the tissue or cereal box?

I was interviewing an executive with a six billion dollar organization. When I shared with her these job search strategies, she confirmed my findings.

"Frequently potential employees send me a résumé. HR usually is not in the loop yet, because I have not informed them of a low achiever. If the résumé looks good and they have applied online, I'll have HR schedule an interview. And frequently, I'll replace the underperformer with such a candidate," she said.

WILLIE
What do you have to lose by contacting a department head or supervisor?

Frankly, most employers are looking for topnotch candidates. In today's economy, it is more important than ever to excel at what you do. Never be satisfied with mediocrity. Let your résumé advertise your successes.

4. WHAT SALARY CAN I EXPECT?

A few years ago, a company in our area was recognized on all the lists as the fastest growing company and best place to work. They took their employees on exotic vacations as a reward. The company expanded rapidly. I suggested to my clients, "If you are being paid above the market salary, save…save…save. Anything that goes up this quickly is likely to come down with equal velocity." Unfortunately, after a few short years the company collapsed. Then I heard, "I wish I had saved more."

Salary is relative. One company pays almost six figures, but they work their managers eighty hours per week. Others pay half as much and have a forty-five-hour workweek. Before you negotiate salary, it is important to know the employer's expectations.

Today, you can look online for salary parameters in other cities and across town. Employers have budgets—some pay above industry standards and others pay substandard wages.

I was on a panel when one of the hiring managers said, "I expect the candidate to negotiate with me. If he accepts my first offer, his negotiation skills may need to be polished."

You will encounter sales managers and purchasing managers who take the above view. Other department heads may give you a more concrete range with no wiggle room.

5. How do I apply online and capture the attention of the hiring authority?

Less than three percent of candidates find employment online. If you are using the online methods, you may find yourself very discouraged. An observation that I make is:

During tough times, human resource recruiters create and hide behind the technology wall.

Candidates seeking employment hide behind their own wall, which is viewing the employment picture through a computer monitor or cell phone.

Technology walls can be frustrating, demoralizing, and cause one to almost give up. Break out of your comfort zone, reach out and communicate with people who can help you achieve your goals. While I don't have a position in my company, I could have a friend and be able to make a connection.

Competition is tough. During a recessionary cycle, I was talking with a recruiter friend who shared the story of a local company that received 1,200 résumés each week and the time demands it placed on the HR staff. It takes hours to screen and evaluate résumés. Can you compete with tired eyes and the flood of résumés?

Competition is brutal! The ant farm is looking better every day.

During the holiday season at the end of 2009, I interviewed a professional with a master's degree in education. He was coachable. He had been looking for a job for over six months while using the internet feverishly. I suggested a low-tech way for finding his next job. I told him to continue applying online. Then, use his strengths, which were relationship building and communication, to locate his next job.

As I mapped out a strategy, he looked at me as if I were old school in my approach to job search. He thought, "How could a career professional be so uninformed?" But what did he have to lose since his way was not working for him?

Initially, I suggested a portfolio, but it was out of his budget. I wanted to help him get his foot in the door with a good organization, so we decided on a traditional two-page résumé.

Trying to be diplomatic, he said, "I thought you were crazy. I contacted the first potential employer and got a fifteen-minute interview. After doing more research, I contacted the next organization on my list, but the decision makers were unavailable. However, the third place I contacted, I asked for three to five minutes of the hiring authority's time and ended up with a forty-five-minute interview. After the second interview, I was hired. I start to work on January 4th, at the salary range I expected. You told me that I might only need five or six résumés after I had submitted hundreds, and I couldn't believe the success."

WILLIE 

Any activity is better than no activity.

6. HOW DO I EXPLAIN NEGATIVE EXPERIENCES OR GAPS IN MY WORK HISTORY?

My first rule is to ignore it on paper. Sometimes this is impossible to accomplish. Take the meth dealer with a $250K per month operation who had spent thirteen years at the state's expense. How do you hide thirteen years? He did manage a high-risk business, didn't he?

One of my clients asked, "How do I explain a three-year gap in my employment?"

"Tell me about it."

"I worked for a company that went public and I took a buyout. Then I bought a boat and sailed the Caribbean for three years. Now, I am ready to go back to work."

"You have great skills. I think they might be jealous, don't you?"

Moms returning to work present gaps as well. This is where you can highlight your volunteer leadership positions and show multitasking skills.

One of my clients, who became a successful recruiter, was such an example. I reframed her résumé while omitting dates. Then she began getting interviews and she would hear, "Why did you omit the dates?"

To which she replied, "We would not be here discussing my background had you seen the gaps in my employment."

This takes finesse and more than just omitting the dates. It takes language that will pique employer's interest.

From time-to-time, I see candidates who have a degree in one area and a career in a totally different sector. One such candidate was a former auditor for the ATF and DEA Federal agencies. She had an English degree along with thirty-plus credit hours of accounting and auditing. She moved to Tulsa from the East Coast. She submitted over fifty résumés and had one interview. When I told her she would need less than ten résumés to land a good job in the area, she looked at me as though I just did not understand the challenges of the current job market. Reluctantly, she wrote the check and later I drafted the résumé. She sent six or seven résumés and had four interviews and three job offers.

WILLIE

Something is not working. Do we continue on this path?

7. How do I know if the company is a good fit for me?

Companies and candidates make missteps frequently. From the candidate's perspective, they presume they can fit in anywhere. Employers believe they can mold candidates into their culture.

DISSIE

I want the most money for the least work.

I was at a meeting with customer service managers from leading airline, insurance, staffing, and retail companies, among others. Before the meeting, we were discussing whether customer service representatives are born or made.

There was one dissenting voice from a car rental company, who said, "We have an excellent training program, which turns out good CRSs."

And I said, "I need to think about this during the meeting." After processing the information, I discovered that I never hired anyone who did not have good customer service skills.

Most managers realize instinctively, that it is easier to build upon the desire to provide effective customer service than to develop those skills from scratch.

As you interview, you want to find the right fit. Do your core values align with those of the targeted company? Have you read their mission statement and values statement?

 **DISSIE**

Are jobs supposed to fit like your house slippers or your favorite pair of gloves?

At a meeting, I was shown a mug shot of an executive caught up in a scandal. The height line showed six foot three inches while the bottom of the picture showed six foot for his height. He was standing on his tiptoes. Dishonesty was pervasive throughout his company.

Would a company managed by the above individual be a good fit for you?

Some companies use assessment tests to determine compatibility.

You must do your due diligence, if you want to be a good fit.

What three things will make a company a good fit for you?

———————————————————————

———————————————————————

———————————————————————

8. How do I explain the bankruptcy, company closing, or downsizing of an employer or multiple employers?

Admittedly, it says something about your judgment when you attach your career star to a declining organization. Why would you join a company in decline? However, it also says you want to contribute to turning around such an organization. You are not afraid of tough decisions and taking risks.

I am used to seeing closed or bankrupt companies crop up on a client's résumé. Working for a troubled company could say something about your judgment. You have the ability to show your resilience by facing the challenges of a changing economic climate.

WILLIE
Analyzing and taking calculated risks will make
you stronger.

A Thought-Provoking Point of View: Companies face
economic challenges from time-totime. An international
business consultant was sharing his story with me about
a consulting assignment in South America. He had been
called in to assess the viability of an unhealthy company.
After an in-depth analysis, his team made recommendations
to restore the company to profitability by slashing jobs.

After developing a detailed business plan and presenting
their findings to the management team, he thought his
assignment was over. Instead, he was given the task of
personally realigning the workforce and terminating
employees.

One day his heart was heavy because he had to terminate a
mom-to-be. In the back of his mind he asked, "Wasn't there
a better way to restore the health of the company?" In fact,
this troubled him for months, which turned into years.

Several months after moving on to a new assignment, he
was reading in the Wall Street Journal that the company
was showing signs of improvement, but had not turned the

financial corner. The decision lingered in the back of his mind for several years, until one day, he received a clipping from a newspaper with no return address.

The brief article stated the company was doing good things in the community. New employees were hired and the company was healthy. "Now I know it was the right thing to do. But it was agonizing until the next chapter was written and the company was strong once again."

WILLIE
Tough decisions are for those making the big bucks.

9 . How do I interview effectively?

Interview preparation is one of the many dots that must be connected. This is no place to let fear or lack of preparation torpedo your efforts. Preparation, clear communication, and planning are among others. You are interviewing the company as much as the company is interviewing you. If "winging it" is your first inclination, because it has always worked for you in the past, you may want to rethink your "No Plan" approach.

Interviewing is all about preparation. *Do you want more than a job that pays the bills?* If your answer is yes, prepare a few answers to common interview questions. But don't read your answers off of the back of your mind as you respond to the interviewer's questions. Engage the interviewer and show your interest and drive.

If you want to enter the path that offers skill-building potential, decision-making opportunities, and the ability to stretch your capabilities, it is important that you communicate to the employer your work style, dedication, and sincere interest in the company. Armed with the appropriate education, intellectual capabilities, energy, and drive, you can create a job for yourself that will position you for a lifetime of promotion. First, you want to look at your background and identify ten questions that you anticipate potential employers will ask. In addition, you want to do this before you send the first résumé.

Some recruiters and department heads like the "Star" approach to interviewing where you identify a situation, task, action, and results of a project or situation. This gives the interviewer insight into your strategic thinking and work style.

Your lack of preparation for the interview may become a roadblock to landing your next job or your "perfect job." Employers state that many candidates are unprepared for the interview. Do your homework, if you plan to succeed. You will find more information in chapter six.

10. Is going back to school and training for another career an option?

Frequently, I see clients transferring from one industry to another after retraining. A few stories come to mind.

There was the registered nurse who went back to school to get an accounting degree. She wanted to work for a consulting firm specializing in the medical industry. She was successful in her pursuits.

There was the warehouse and distribution manager who went back to school to become a registered nurse. Here again he made a smooth transition.

Chiropractor, Dr. Ronald Bergman, tells the story that was the driving force for him to enroll in a chiropractic college. His dad was a plumber in New Jersey and Ron was about thirteen years old. One cold, snowy day, his dad dropped him off at a local restaurant to unplug a sewer. He worked to unclog the drain for what seemed like hours, but he couldn't move the sewer cap. Ready to give up, he decided to give it one more try before his dad returned. The pressure was so intense that it knocked him back on the snow-covered pavement. Now he was cold, stinky, and beginning to shiver. He knocked on the restaurant door. "Stinky, you can't come into the kitchen smelling like that." Several minutes later, his dad arrived on the scene, but not before he made the decision to go to school and not become a plumber.

WILLIE

Education and training will provide return on investment unless you have an entitlement mentality.

I also remember a customer service manager going back to school to get an advertising and public relations degree, who became very bitter about her limited career choices.

Then there was the producer for National Public Radio who pre-interviewed national newsmakers who completed a legal assisting program. She wanted to move to Colorado and join a law firm. The last time we visited she was in dialog with law firms in the area.

One client wanted to move to Israel and work in a major hotel. She asked, "Do I need a degree to get there?" I suggested that she go to the local community college and ask about their program. As a non-traditional student, when exploring any higher education program, ask to speak to the professor who oversees the program and a graduate in the field. I also suggested that she ask the starting pay with a degree. Then I recommended that she schedule an appointment with the human resource director of a major hotel to elicit career advancement opportunities and salary information. Then, she should ask what the salary range would be after graduating with a two-year degree.

Education and training are two of the keys to launching a good career. One of my clients is a high school guidance counselor. She found it necessary to tell the students to select a university with a good program that supported their life goal. She had a student that wanted to study meteorology and was applying to Oklahoma State University. The high school counselor asked, "Why haven't you applied to the University of Oklahoma—the number-one meteorology program in the nation?" "Because my friends are attending OSU." WRONG ANSWER!

Recap

It doesn't matter the program. Do you have a list of basic questions to ask of any admissions representative? What are the talents required to be successful in the academic program? In the career? How much does the average graduate earn? Is there a demand for graduates? Remember, you don't want to gain admittance into a program that goes the way of boot manufacturing, buggy-whip making, or a technology that is obsolete.

11. How long do I remain in a job that is a bad fit?

Another dot that must be connected is stability. Most employers expect employees to remain on the job for two to five years. Employers understand that employee turnover is costly. I look at every job as an opportunity to learn something. Perhaps I am performing under my skill level, but I am adding to my personal toolbox. When looking at my personal career in the rearview mirror, each job prepared me in some way for the next. Some of the most boring jobs that I held taught me the most.

Staying employed with an employer for two to five years will show a stable work history. The exceptions might be if you are in personal jeopardy, you are asked to compromise your values or other such similar conditions.

WILLIE 
Approach each new job as a learning experience.

12. How do I keep a job once I get it?

Presuming that you want to keep the job, find someone respected in the organization and see if he or she will mentor you. Do a good job. Ask for special projects. You may ask what skills you need to develop in order to be of more value to the company. Take classes on your own time. If the company has an online university, read the material, obtain certifications, and become an expert in your area.

WILLIE
Become a content expert.

Twelve Frequently Asked Questions by Job Seekers in a Soft Economy

1. How can I support myself in a bad economy?

2. What are my most marketable skills?

3. Who is hiring in times like these?

4. What salary can I expect?

5. How do I apply online to capture the attention of the hiring authority?

6. How do I explain negative experiences or gaps in my work history?

7. How do I know if the company is a good fit for me?

8. How do I explain the bankruptcy, company closing or downsizing of an employer or multiple employers?

9. How do I interview effectively?

10. Should I go back to school to obtain more training?

11. How long do I remain in a job that is a bad fit?

12. How do I keep a job once I get it?

Eleven Career Stories

1

Larry came into my office at the end of May 2006. He had just returned from Saudi Arabia a few days earlier and had lived in the complex in Riyadh. It was the site of the May 16, 2006 bombing. He was visibly shaken. He talked about the ordeal that is beyond human comprehension. I listened and did not ask any questions. When he came back to pick up his résumé, Larry told me his story.

For the first forty-seven years of his life, he had lived on the family farm or been a farmer in Arkansas, except for a brief tour of duty with the United States Air Force where he was an aircraft mechanic. But farming was his life. His family did not own the land—only leased it. As a new generation of landowners inherited the land, they decided to lease the land to another farmer who had convinced them he could make more money for the landholders.

As Larry told the story of how his father and uncle had farmed the land, you could feel his passion for farming. After his uncle died, he joined his father in the farming operations. His life was good until one day when he received a letter terminating the lease agreement. There was no discussion. The decision was final. All the personal property and farming equipment were liquidated.

His wife asked him, "What do you want to do now?"

He told her, "I have always wanted to work on airplanes."

"What do we need to do?"

"I need to attend Spartan School of Aeronautics and get Air Frame and Power Plant licenses."

With that decision, they packed their belongings and moved to Tulsa. Larry attended school and worked full-time. The day of graduation, the vice president of the school said, "Larry, I would like to talk with you in my office, before you leave today."

The administrator offered Larry a teaching position and he taught Aircraft Maintenance. He was later offered the position in Riyadh and lived abroad for two years. At fifty-seven, Larry once again was looking for a new career. He polished his résumé and had an interview in Little Rock within a few days.

WILLIE 
A career change can happen when you least expect it!

2

Johnny came to see me after losing his job with a large candy manufacturer following a downsizing. It wasn't difficult for him to find a sales job, but it was a challenge to find the "right" sales fit. His goal was to work for the number one positioned product—not the number two positioned product in the market. He interviewed with the number one gum manufacturer in a local market and even paid his own way for an interview to the east coast, but didn't land the job. Naturally, he was disappointed, but he kept in contact with the decision makers. After a management change, he again applied and this time the new manager wanted someone with experience—someone who needed no training or handholding through the transition. This company that had overlooked a top performer was in a position to hire a top-notch employee who could hit the ground running. It took time, persistence, and patience. Johnny was rewarded with a position with a leading company.

WILLIE
Set your goals high so you can stretch your potential.

3

One of my clients worked her way through college as an assistant manager and retail manager for a scrapbook company. She was passionate about the product and the benefits of the hobby for her customers. After graduating from college, she landed a territory sales position with the leading scrapbook supplier. Promotions were soon to follow. She conducted training programs and was an expert for the company. She was a success in every way.

My phone rings, "Vicki, my dreams have changed. I have met someone. I want to settle down and have a family. This job will no longer work for me. Help me. My passion and goals have changed!"

WILLIE 
Dreams change! New dreams emerge!

4

Sometime around Christmas 2000, I was contacted by an individual employed by a large telecommunications company. She had earned a degree and was seeking advancement opportunities, but didn't know what her superiors wanted to see on a self-evaluation form. She was stuck in a dead end position. We discussed her successes from the previous year and then showcased her accomplishment on the form that the company provided. I didn't give it much thought, that is, until the next year around the same time. She called again, "I need your help. Last year I got the promotion, and I want another one this year."

So again, I framed her successes around what the company required. When she left my office she said, "Merry Christmas, I'll see you next year."

A few years later, I was visiting with a human resource professional from the same organization and we were discussing career advancement within organizations. This HR executive was explaining how the company qualifies candidates for promotion. Supervisors look through a unique lens to determine if their employees can communicate and analyze effectively before they are promoted to the next level, because the company promotes managers who communicate well.

It is vital to understand the screening tools used by your company, so you can be effective at leveraging opportunity and obtaining promotions. Your company may look at these same benchmarks or they may have a totally different list.

WILLIE
The best position may be with your current employer.

5

A pharmaceutical sales representative, who is a client, updates his brag book* that showcases his accomplishments frequently along with his résumé. He was in a coffee shop in a major hotel chain and observed that a pharmaceutical sales organization was conducting interviews.

When he saw a brief break, he walked up to the recruiter and very politely asked, "Would you consider one more interview later today?" Then he presented a copy of his résumé.

He was uncertain of the answer to his special request, but the recruiter responded, "Can you be back at 3:30 p.m. today?"

Not only was he back at the appointed time, but he had his updated brag book* in hand. He was selected for the position. The last time he updated his résumé, he was the number-one ranked sales representative in the nation for the company. That minor intrusion on the time of the recruiter and his preparedness provided the platform for the ongoing success for both my client and the company, which he now represents.

*A brag book is a collection of letters, e-mails, awards, and statistical information validating your successes.

WILLIE
Always be prepared with an up-todate résumé and portfolio. Always!

6

A registered nurse with supervisory and management experience in psych units had left her career to care for her aging parents. Her professional responsibilities with the job included supervising, budgeting, and operations, but family needs interrupted her career. She organized siblings and coordinated all care giving. When she decided to return to work, she wanted a professional résumé and cover letter to connect the dots. As she and I discussed, she could walk into any hospital in America and get a job, but she wanted more than just a job, she wanted to restart her career. I explained that sometimes my clients could make the move in one step and in other times, it might take two steps to land a promising career position. We discussed salary and we kicked around an acceptable salary range. A few weeks later, she walked into my office with a big smile on her face.

She had an offer on the table. "I wanted to let you know that I've got a good job in Dallas making about $7,000 more than we expected with great perks. The résumé opened the right doors."

WILLIE 
Have a plan and expect the best outcome!

7

A single mom who is a successful sales rep took a job that required extensive overtime. She was confident in her sales abilities and went on to take a position with fewer demands. "I only have three more years of parenting. Then I can pursue a more demanding position." One sales manager was impressed with her qualifications and said, "Everything I need to see is right here on her résumé. She will be an asset to my team. I'm sure she will make me money, even with her parenting responsibilities."

WILLIE
Life happens!

Linda came into the office when unemployment in her industry was at its peak. I explained what I could do for her. She told me, "I have $450 in my checking account and one more paycheck. Do I really need this résumé and cover letter?"

Because of my training, I said, "Yes, you do."

But then I began to second-guess myself before she came back to the office to pick up her résumé. The conversation that I was having with myself went something like, "Are you taking advantage of the unemployed? Are you sure this will work for your client?"

About one in ten clients follow up with me after an interview. Linda was one of the clients who called to tell me about the interview. Her interview was before e-mail so she submitted résumés via snail mail. When she arrived for the fifteen-minute interview the recruiter pointed to his credenza where he had four stacks of résumés two feet high and said, "You are one of 1,500 candidates applying for this job and your résumé is the best that we received. The job is yours if you want it."

A few years later, Linda needed an update and went to an office in Dallas. She asked the writer if he knew Vicki from Tulsa and he told her that he was going to be in a meeting with me in a few weeks.

Linda said, "Please tell Vicki that my career has been on track since my initial investment. I have never regretted for one minute compiling a professional résumé and investing in the service."

WILLIE
Understand the difference in an extravagant purchase and an investment in your future.

9

During the spring of 2005, a prospect walked into my office and we talked. Then I said, "What do you want to do?" Meaning what type of position interests you most. He could not give me a definitive answer. We talked in general about opportunities. Frankly, he was not focused. And I told him, "I am afraid you will not be successful with your job search since you don't know what you want to do. It is a lot like going duck hunting at night and not knowing where the ducks are. You can make a lot of racket but not achieve success."

He claimed that I sent him on his way without taking his money. Now that doesn't sound like me, but... A few months later he came back to see me and said, "You were helpful before and I have been thinking about what you said.

But first, I am going to write you a check and pay you."

This time, as we talked, he had a clear picture of what he wanted to do. While he had more than one focus, he had direction and I drafted a résumé for him. He was moving to Missouri.

WILLIE

> If you don't have any idea of what you want to do in your work life, talk to someone who can give you guidance. *You may need to visit a career counselor or consultant.*

10

A mechanical engineer in his early fifties came in for a technical résumé. The job market was weak and we had been talking at least once a week by phone discussing career options. He had questions regarding how he could transition to a new company. He came by my office after about six weeks and said, "I can't find anything on the Internet or in newspaper."

I said, "If you've got a minute, let me take a look online for you.

To both of our amazement, over fifteen engineering positions had been posted online in our area within the past twenty-four hours. This was very encouraging. Randomly, I selected one of the positions and asked, "How many companies are there in Tulsa that would advertise for this position?"

"There are about thirteen or so major players that could use a mechanical engineer with these skills."

"What I recommend is that you go to the phonebook or industry directory and get the names and addresses of the owners or general managers of the companies and snail mail your résumé to each of the decision makers. Then, after about three days, begin making phone calls to the companies. After three for four phone calls, you may uncover who is hiring within your industry. If not, make a few more phone calls. Then you will know where to follow up aggressively." By chance, you may uncover other positions by asking, "Do you know anyone in the industry who is hiring?"

I just as easily could have said, pick up the phone and contact the decision makers. But first develop a telephone presentation to uncover who is hiring and what level of interest there is in the industry, or obtain e-mail addresses and begin communication with someone in the company.

WILLIE 
Was this timing or luck?

Bonus

It is necessary to mine for information, conduct research, and analyze data from various sources in order to focus on useable data for a successful job search.

11

On another occasion, I was leading a professional team-building meeting. The number one sales associate in the company was on a losing streak.

"Sue, tell me what happened.

Slumped over in the chair with no confidence and a shaky voice, she said, "I had a client who told me I was stupid and that I didn't know what I was doing. With his words, he did everything he could do to destroy me personally and professionally. I can't get over it."

"What have you done to get over the slump?"

"I have relived each word of our conversation to uncover what I did wrong. I'm off my game."

"Sue, tell me about one of your successful clients."

As she told her success story, she sat up straight, her voice took on a confident tone, and she became animated.

"Sue, I want you to write that story down on a piece of paper. And why not reach into your memory banks and write a few more stories where your clients added $10,000 to their annual salaries. Each morning read these stories. Begin playing your good memories in your head."

A few weeks later, I was reviewing the sales standing list. Sue's name was once again at the top of the list of 500 or so of her peers. When I saw her later, she said, "I'm playing the good memories—it's working. Thank you!"

WILLIE

"Recall your successes and learn from them."

Write your success stories below:

____

____

____

____

____

____

____

Ten Forms That You May Find Helpful

YOU WILL FIND TEN FORMS in the following pages. The first is a checklist of tools you may need to obtain a new position. The second is a list of potential headings for your résumé. The third form has many uses as listed in items three through seven. These examples will help you target careers that interest you the most. Then, you will find printed forms including an Accomplishment Inventory, Achievement Memorandum, Job Search Contact Plan & Schedule, Interview Preparation Work Sheet, and Job Search Matrix. You may want to develop something on your computer to capture the information or use these forms.

1. Job Search Check List

2. Résumé Heading

3. The primary way that I use the eight lines are for eight different positions that interest you and list potential companies in the outer area

4. Use four of the eight lines closest to the center to list: Strengths, Weaknesses, Obstacles, and Opportunities (you may want to do both a self-evaluation and have a friend/mentor complete the same list)

5. Or, in the same vein, use the eight lines to list the industries that interest you and then list the companies with the potential to hire you

6. Another use may be helpful in developing a Life Plan using the eight lines for: Short Term Financial/Long-term Financial, Career, Health and Fitness, Relationship/Family, Education/Continuing Education, Philanthropic/Charity, Spiritual, Leisure, and list your goals in the outer area

7. For federal jobs, list the agencies which can use your skills and search USAjobs.com for locations and positions posted

Forms three and four were designed because we have information overload. We could do a quick search and uncover hundreds of jobs and companies, and frantically begin to apply online. When applying for any and everything, there is no focus to your search. You need a starting point to systemize the information between our thoughts and the keyboard. These forms are designed to give you clarity.

Being overwhelmed with information is, in many cases, an understatement. This simple form helps our clients walk through the process of what they want to do at this time and place with their work life.

Many of the people I see are in career transition. They may simply be unemployed, seeking a job in a challenging economic climate or they may be reinventing themselves. *I recommend that you use a pencil with an eraser.*

Over the course of a day or two, complete the form, identifying those companies or industries that interest you the most. Then, let the greatest sorting mechanism of all time, "your brain," sort through your options.

You will be able to identify the career choices that interest you the most. Then, define your objectives and begin your search. Also, you will be able to mark off your distractions.

You will be able to use this form to narrow or expand job search parameters.

List Eight Position Titles that Interest You

____

____

____

List Eight Industries or Companies that Interest You

You can make a copy of Appendix A

Job Search Check List

Date Prepared/Revised_________

☐ Brief Résumé—one page

☐ Expanded Version of Résumé—two to three pages

☐ Portfolio

☐ Cover Letter

☐ Letter of Resignation

☐ Broadcast Letter

☐ Thank You for the Interview Letter

☐ Follow Up Letter

☐ Bio (brief)

☐ Reference List

☐ Writing Samples

☐ Picture(s)

☐ Tax Return

☐ Driving Record

☐ Credit Report

☐ Statistical Information

☐ Performance Verification

☐ 30/60/90 Day Plan

☐ Five Reasons to Hire Me

☐ Performance Matrices

☐ Professional Voice Mail Recording

☐ Professional E-mail Address

TYPICAL INFORMATION AND HEADING USED FOR RÉSUMÉ DEVELOPMENT

You will need to select the appropriate heading for your individual résumé.

Contact Information
Name
Address
Phone
E-mail

Objective

Profile

Summary

Qualification Brief

Professional Experience

Work Experience

Special Projects

Practicum

Internship

Education

Course Concentration

Continuing Education

Affiliations

Professional Organizations

Civic & Community Organizations

Certificates & Licenses

Awards and Honors

References Available Upon Request

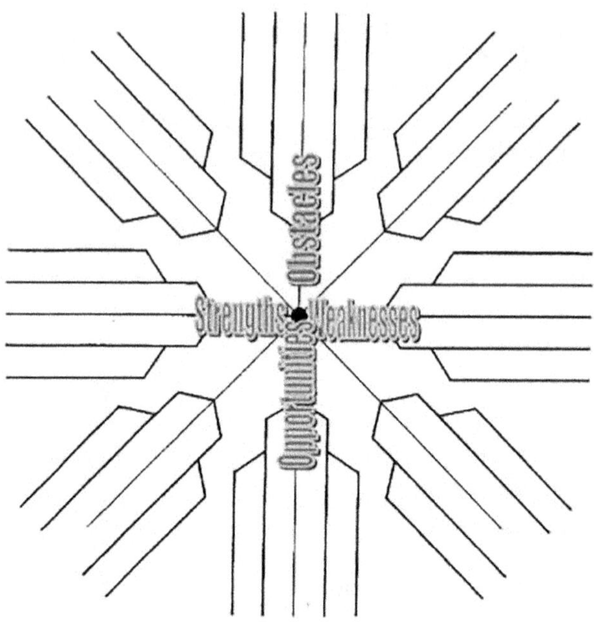

You can identify your strengths, weaknesses, opportunities, and obstacles to employment. You can build your template to address your specific needs.

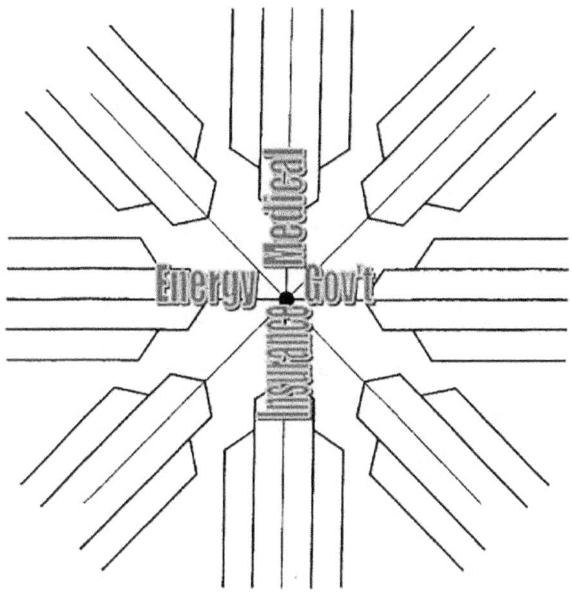

You can list the industries that interest you the most and replace energy with (Exxon, Conoco Phillips, Shell, British Petroleum), medical (local hospitals, bio medical firms, pharmaceutical companies, specialty hospitals), insurance (BlueCross Blue Shield, United Health Care, Aetna, Community Care), and government (various federal, state, and local facilities) with any industry you choose. Then list the organizations in your area that interest you.

There is a blank in Appendix A

Accomplishment Inventory

During my career, the three accomplishments I am most proud of are:

____

____

____

____

____

____

During my career, I have contributed to the efficiency/improvement of operations by:

____

____

____

During my career, I have contributed to saving the company money by:

During my career, I have contributed to making the company money by:

During my career, I have contributed to the community by:

____

____

____

____

____

Achievement Memorandum

Achievement:

The Situation Before I Became Involved:

How My Involvement Came About:

What Did I Do?

Why Did I Do It That Way?

Most Satisfying Thing About This Accomplishment:

One Thing I Would Do Different / One Thing I Learned From This:

Job Search Contact Plan
And Schedule For:

Name: Day/Date: /

INTERVIEWS TODAY

Time	Comany	Position	Notes

8:30-10 am   Marketing Calls

Company	Contact	Phone	Outcome

10 am-10:45 am   "Touching Base" Calls

Name	Phone	From	Notes

11 am-Noon   Correspondence

Company	Contact	Type of Correspondence	Notes

12:30-2:30 pm | Research & Prospecting Calls

Company	Phone	Main Contact	Other Contact 1	Other Contact 2

2:30-3:30 pm   Preparing First-Time Mail Outs

Company	Address	Sent To	Source

3:30-5 pm   Follow Up Calls

Name	Purpose/ Company	Phone	Notes

5-5:30 pm

Organize Today's
Information/Prepare for Tomorrow

Interview Preparation Worksheet

Company Name:

____

Interview Number:

____

Address:

____

____

Interview Date:

____

Day:

____

Time:

____

Interview with:

____

Title:

____

Telephone:

____

Position Interviewing for:

____

This company is engaged in:

____

As I understand it, this position requires:

____

Other things I know about this organization:

____

____

____

My experience that best prepares me for this position is:

____

My accomplishments that will contribute to success in this position are:

____

____

____

____

____

My education/training that will contribute to success in this position is:

____

____

The skills that best suit me for this position are:

____

____

____

____

Examples of my abilities that I plan to use in the interview are:

____

____

____

____

Questions I plan to ask about the position include:

____

The "marketing" statement I plan to use (accomplishments, experience/skills/education):

____

____

____

____

____

____

Job Search Matrix

Task	Points	Mon.	Tues.	Wed.	Thurs.	Fri.
Internet Research	1 point for each Company					
Application	5 points for each Application					
Informational Interview/ Touch Point	1 point for each by phone, email, direct mail					
Follow-Up	1 point					
Telephone Interview	1 point if negative; 5 points if positive					
Face-to-Face Interview	5 points if negative; 10 points if positive					
Offer	25 points					
Totals						

To fast track your job search, set your goal as 100 points each day.

Nine Basics of
Résumé Development

Presentation and packaging are key factors in any marketing endeavor, especially when your résumé is the marketing material that will move your career to the next level. The plethora of expert advice can be both overwhelming and intimidating—particularly when the advice forcefully recommends only one page, a certain font, paper color, or magic potion. Some of the experts have a recruiter's point of view, others an executive, human resource, or business specialty background. Some look through the lens of their own corporate culture. It could be the lens of an industrial psychologist or it could be from the perspective of "will you be a good fit for us?" Even a legal compliance viewpoint makes its way to the decision-making process. Career experts have written volumes and daily there are new tips on the internet about job search. While all are valid from their individual perspective, the advice can be overpowering and plant thoughts of inadequacy into the most confident professional.

I have given talks on résumé development. Yes, I can teach the mechanics, but not the distinguishing traits that make a good résumé and outstanding, high-impact, over-the-top presentation while still leaving room to make an exceptional impression at the interview. Everyone brings a unique set of skills, personality, and energy to potential positions. Writing about this individual is as distinctive as your fingerprint.

One of my clients wanted to relocate to Los Angeles. He sold his business in northeastern Oklahoma and investigated new career opportunities on the west coast. His aunt worked as an executive assistant for the CEO of Disney. My insecurities surfaced and my mind danced with thoughts of, "Would my client's résumé impress the company that entertains us with imagination and wonder?" When my phone rang, the client rather sternly said, "I need to talk with you. I am in Tulsa and I'll be in your office in fifteen minutes." My first thought was that the "Typo Queen" had struck again.

When he walked in to my office he said, "I had to promise my aunt that I would come back to your office and tell you what she said about your work." His tone was not complimentary. So I presumed the worst and that he wanted a refund.

After reviewing his résumé, she told him, "Your résumé is one of the top five that has ever crossed my desk. Where did you have it done?"

"Tulsa," he answered.

"Oklahoma?" She went on to tell him that if he could have gotten that quality in Los Angeles, it would have cost him over $1,500. "Promise me that when you get back to Oklahoma, you will tell the writer what I have said. Her work is outstanding."

WILLIE 

Is it time for you to beat you own drum?

Several factors impact the effectiveness of your résumé. If the unemployment rate is above acceptable levels, it may be difficult to land an interview even with the best résumé. If the unemployment rate is extremely low, you could get an interview with your qualifications written on a brown paper bag or a paper plate.

Many résumé evaluators spend less than ten seconds reviewing your qualifications. Online résumés are scanned for key words and individuals exercise the delete key. They spend less than three seconds with many documents before making a decision about your future. During the downturn of 2008-2012, companies are receiving hundreds of résumés for one opening. It takes time to evaluate each résumé. Last year one major international company received almost one million résumés for two thousand openings. Fifty percent of the applicants did not meet minimal requirements according to a *Wall Street Journal* story. You will find compelling career information in the Tuesday edition of the *Wall Street Journal.*

Whether you are packaging your résumé for online readers, an advertised position, or a networking opportunity, it is important to understand what the reader wants to see on your résumé. This may be a daunting task where the requirements may be as unique as a fingerprint or like the perfect fit of your favorite gloves.

The résumé has your name and contact information including phone numbers and e-mail addresses. Some of the early templates in a leading software package positioned this information in very small print and in a font that was not easy to read. If your purpose is to get a phone call or e-mail response, make sure this information is easy to find and read.

Next, you will want to set the tone for what the reader will find in your qualifications, while piquing their interest and distinguishing yourself from the other candidates. You will need to set up headings including work experience and education. If you are active in community organizations, you will need to make a heading for affiliations.

Additionally, you will need to develop a method to highlight your honors and achievements, so the interviewer can see in their mind's eye what you have accomplished. You want the interviewer to immediately connect the dot of what you have done in your past with the dot of what you can contribute to the organization. The words that you use will reflect your character, work style and, in many cases, identify whether you are bragging or possess the work ethic that is required to be successful in the position. An effective résumé will demonstrate your skills, accent your potential, and reflect more than your past.

WILLIE

Self-promotion can be good. If you need a professionally written résumé to advance your career, have one written.

"The worst career mistake that I have made in years was not writing you a check the first day we met. I put it off and have been stressed for several months now," said a former pharmacy owner. He went on to say, "It took me only a few days to find the right position after you drafted my résumé. I had struggled for months while missing the mark of what employers wanted to see."
You can't discuss résumés without incorporating into the discussion the length of the résumé. Some experts feel strongly a one-page is best. Still others want more information before making an educated decision prior to the interview process. An argument can be made for a one-page in some situations.

If you have less than six years of experience, you may only need a one-page format. Some job seekers with a stable work history with one employer can get by with a one page. A lengthier career history may be in order for others depending on your accomplishments and successes.

 Only use a one-page résumé!

 No use a portfolio!

 I like my six pages detailing my one job.

 Mine is perfect. It is printed on lavender paper

I had a discussion with an owner of a recruiting firm. He said, "You don't like a one-page only format, do you?"

"Actually, I prefer taking as much space as needed to tell the story of my clients' history. Usually, that is no more than two pages, sometimes a little longer for someone with more than twenty years of experience and strong accomplishments," I responded.

Professionals in medicine and academics may need a curriculum vitae or executive presentation to tell their story effectively to committees and boards. Biographies are valuable for presenters and business leaders.

Language and style can change depending upon the company that is receiving your résumé and other factors in the corporate culture. Hot jargon might be used in one decade and considered blasé in another. It is important to know and understand industry jargon. Companies have internal lexicon as well that may or may not translate across competitive organizations.

I realize there are many résumé and career experts. Some write from the perspective of a human resource director of a global company or even business owners. Several write from a government helping agency perspective. There are department heads with specialized expertise in various disciplines. Others write from a recruiter's point-of-view. Several write from a temporary employment agency perspective. Still others have written a couple of résumés with success and they want to share their knowledge. Some write from a historical perspective, "this is about your past accomplishments." A professional résumé writer gets a picture of what you want to accomplish and writes to that objective. At the same time, the professional résumé writer draws from industry language, local expectations, shifts in the economy, and business trends to build your résumé. As the client, you will find the process a team effort. If you're not confused yet, read a couple of articles online, pick up several books at the library, or visit your local bookstore.

WILLIE
Everyone is an expert! It can be a challenge determining which advice will work for me.

Time and time again, I hear, "I have wrestled with this for two weeks and can't get it right. Help! I'm confused."

Bonus

After you get your résumé fine-tuned, you will also need to collect a list of *references*. Contact your references, obtain their permission, and tell them to expect calls from potential employers. You will need three to five references. Select only people who will provide credible information about you. Offer to send your résumé to each reference that you selected.

If you are moving to a new city, you may want to request reference letters from people who can speak to your work ethic, character, and qualifications.

I recommend that you *select references* that see your skill set, professionalism, and work style from several perspectives. If you are a member of an organization and you serve on the board, you may want to use a contact from the organization.

You may want to use a customer, vendor, or respected business leader to round out your reference list. Some managers like to see a supervisor, peer, and subordinate.

You want to *disseminate your reference* information to only organizations that interest you the most. I was interviewing a writer several years ago. To impress me and other employers, she had the name and private numbers of the state's governor and US senators. For a moment, I was impressed. Then I realized, when she told me she wasn't interested in the position, it would have been more professional to have treated her references with more discretion and guarded their personal information more carefully.

Letters are crucial in the job search. You may use a *broadcast letter* to summarize your skills and expertise. This letter is sent to many decision makers with the goal of capturing *any* decision-maker's attention.

When there is no response from the employer, the *follow-up letter* is designed to show your ongoing interest in employment in the company and your desire to be an asset to their team.

DISSIE

Perhaps if I stalk the employers, they'll feel sorry
for me and hire me!

WILLIE
Not in this lifetime.

Distinguish yourself by remembering to say thank you by e-mail or snail mail. I usually recommend both. Within hours of the interview, send a thank you e-mail. Follow up with a thank you letter or high-impact thank you card. First, you want to show that you know how to work at the speed of business. Second, you want to show that you understand business protocol. When the candidate pool is distilled to two equally qualified candidates, the appreciative one will be hired every time—unless the candidate shoots himself or herself in the foot.

A recruiter shared a story about a specific thank you note that was sent following an interview that backfired. The offer was ready to be extended to a qualified candidate, until he sent a thank you note on Valentine's Day wallpaper, which his daughter had selected on the home computer. He did not know how to change the wallpaper on the e-mail, and it cost him the job.

The Mechanics of Building a Résumé

- There are templates available for various industries and specific positions.

- Use no more than two fonts on any one document.

- Use bold and font size for headings. Depending on the number of characters in your name use 18 to 24 point font for your name. For heading be consistent. Use the same font as the body or the résumé only one font larger.

- For printed documents, use Times New Roman, Book Antiqua, or Cambria.

- For an online document, use Arial, Tahoma, or Calibri.

- Margins no less than one inch right and left and no less than "point six inches" top and bottom.

- Font size for the name—twenty-point; and résumé body—eleven to twelve point.

- Review for consistency in print/font, format, and appearance.

- Proofread document carefully.

- Have a professional e-mail address and record a professional voicemail.

- Summarize your skills in a brief summary statement.

- Identify technical attributes and expertise.

- Identify interpersonal, communicational, and organizational skills.

- Obtain a list of key words used in your industry—use six to twelve words that are appropriate.

- List your accomplishments.

- Write a description of your duties and responsibilities (four to five sentences).

- Write descriptions to showcase your qualifications.

- Use present tense for current jobs and past tense for other positions.

- Use bullets or a combination of bullets and paragraphs.

- Begin with the most recent job (reverse chronological order).

- Most employers want to see a ten-year work record.

- Employment agencies may want to see a full work history.

- Minimize the use of acronyms—spell out all abbreviations.

- Use action verbs and do not use personal pronouns.

- How was your performance measured?

- Did you resolve problems? How?

- Recent graduates highlight education.

- Experienced workers highlight their experience.

- List continuing education and professional development.

- Arrange information with the most relevant first.

- Headings to consider:
  - Professional Memberships
  - Military
  - License & Certification
  - Foreign Language Fluency
  - Awards & Recognition
  - Community Involvement
  - Experience
  - Education
  - Summary
  - Objective
- Make sure the words are right!

WILLIE

Verify all contact information like your phone and e-mail address.

Résumé Tips

1. Help the résumé reader by providing easy-tofind contact information.
2. Determine the presentation that works best for your industry and region while ensuring a realistic, credible, and confidence-building presentation that illustrates integrity.

3. Know your industry and the jargon, along with key words you would want to see on a résumé. Which words would your supervisor want to see?

4. Walk the line by exemplifying confidence without overstating your success at this stage of your career life.

5. Mechanics, length of résumé, size of font, and print style, among others, impact your final presentation with contributing factors to include: industry, position, and experience level.

6. Economic climates and markets demand a distilled language on your résumé, while integrating strengths, explaining your qualifications, and addressing your ability to impact changing market conditions.

7. By condensing information and using clear language, you can make the résumé a quick read and workable for digital applications.

8. Knowing the audience is vital. There is a difference in writing to technical, management, educational, medical, aerospace, and telecommunications industries.

9. Every good writer needs the best editor. Remember proofreading, spelling, and editing are basic as you prepare the résumé.

Eight Interviewing Pointers

In the previous chapters, we have discussed résumé building, identifying targeted companies, pinpointing your skills, and framing your accomplishments for impact. These are a few more of the dots that you must connect to move your career forward. You have read stories about clients struggling with career concerns. Most of this information is designed to get you to the interview. If you can't get an interview, you will not get a job. Now we are going to discuss the ins and outs of interviewing. At the end of the process, this is where an offer will be made, or you will receive the "thank you for your interest in our company" letter or hear nothing at all.

Most companies are looking for candidates that will work well within their corporate culture, perform above average, and become a content expert. Preparation is the key to successful interviewing.

During the weeks preceding the closing of a call center, a personnel agency asked me to assist with a presentation of job search strategies and tips for interviewing effectively. One of the participants asked how to answer the question, "Why do you want to work here?" A flawless answer rolled off my tongue, "Your company looks for people who know the value of being punctual, communicating clearly, and providing superb customer service. Even more, you are looking for a team member who can sell products and boost profits. I know I can be an asset to your team."

While the HR director was very discreet, out of the corner of my eye, I saw her roll her eyes. But I continued, wanting to make my point clear. I suggested they take notes and speak slowly so they could get every word. Then I said, "'Ms. HR Director,' do you mind sharing with us why you will not hire me?

"Vicki, you are too smooth and have too much practice reciting the answer."

Before you let this story reinforce your lackadaisical, shoot-from-the-hip preparation interview strategy, let's revisit the above story. It was not the answer that triggered the negative response, but it was the delivery. Everything from the tone of your voice, your pitch, your facial expression, and even your posture are elements of the communication process. Many times the decision about hiring you is made before you open your mouth. Traditionally, handshakes are used as a measuring stick as well.

Over twenty years ago, a young manager for a freight company visited with me. There was definitely something special about this young professional, but I could not put my finger on it. He had presence when he walked into the room. Even sitting in a chair, he took command of the interview. As we talked, he told me about completing training in Europe on business presence. He said, "For a week they taught me how to walk into a room and take control."

After visiting with thousands of clients over twenty-five years, I remember his presence as he captured my attention. He made an indelible impression on me, in a good way. During an interview, make it your goal to make such an impression on the interviewer—a good one.

On a visit to Jackson, Mississippi, I encountered a human resource executive, a petite lady, who graduated from college *magna cum laude* at age nineteen, and wanted me to build her résumé. She was bright and navigated her career flawlessly. She recruited sales executives and managers for a leading insurance company and she told me, "I don't put much faith in résumés and even in the interview, because so many of the people that I interview in my industry masquerade as a top performer and talk a good game—performance is another issue. I want to know they're a top performer and only time will tell. Sometimes, the least likely candidates become top performers and the outstanding ones on paper can't make quota."

While this was more than two decades ago, I am confident we would have the same conversation today. It is important that you communicate your successes, but it is more important to surpass expectations.

As you look at your résumé, review your qualifications and shine a laser on each of your weaknesses hiding in the corners of your mind. You need to write down each weakness and the questions that you anticipate being asked. Take a good look at your list.

What question can you imagine the interviewer asking that you have not anticipated?

____

____

____

You can do an internet search for interview questions as well. *While you know you should do the research, you might not, so here is Vicki's list:*

1. What do you want to tell me about yourself? (They don't want to hear that you have six cats, scuba dive, and vacation in Las Vegas. They want to hear and see that you are intelligent and have the ability to make an ongoing commitment to corporate goals.)

2. Who has been an influential role model in your life? And why? (Give this question some thought and how it will be perceived by the interviewer.)

3. Which three words describe you? (Based on research, what do they want to hear? If you have been listening and researched the company, you will pick up on what they want to hear.)

4. Why do you want to work here? How did you learn about this job opening? (If you haven't done your research, that question will become a thorn in your side.)

5. What motivates you?

6. Describe your ideal job.

7. Why did you choose this field?

8. What did you enjoy most about your last position?

9. What are/were you duties?

10. What can you do for us that someone else can't?

11. Were you in the first wave of layoffs?

12. You work for a respected company. Why do you want to change jobs?

13. Do you have references?

14. Do you have a salary history?

15. You're overqualified and wouldn't be happy in the position, would you?

16. Give me an example of an occasion where you did your best.

17. Tell me about two or three of your recent goals and what you did to achieve them.

18. List the books you've read this month. What publications do you read often?

19. What do you expect to be doing five years from today?

20. Do you prefer working with others, in a team, or by yourself?

21. How do you define leadership? Give an example of your leadership style.

22. Tell me about a difficult project you've handled? Was it a team project?

23. How do you deal with criticism, disappointment, or rejection?

24. How effective of a communicator are you? What is the worst communication problem that you have experienced?

25. How do you structure your presentations?

26. Give examples of meeting deadlines.

27. Give examples of working under pressure.

28. Give examples of improving performance. Can you prove it?

29. How do you set priorities and organize your workday?

30. What's your greatest strength? What's your greatest weakness?

31. What are the qualities of a good manager/sales manager/project manager?

32. Recent graduates: What were your favorite classes? Favorite professors?

33. How did you balance your studies with other activities?

34. What do you expect from this position? Why should we hire you?

35. What classes/seminars have you taken, which influenced you the most?

36. Explain what you consider the primary function of this position.

37. Is quality a concern of the position? How do you balance risk and opportunity?

38. How does your prior experience qualify you for this position?

Now, I am going to share with you a secret of successful interviewing. If you will prepare three different answers to each of these questions, you will be competitive in any interview process. Understand that many companies train their interviewers regarding methods for strategically interviewing candidates. These interviewers have a plan; you will need one as well. Some interviewers use best selling interview strategies and "interview by the book."

Everything that I have written about interviewing must be done before you send out your first résumé. You will be behind the curve if you do anything less.

During your research, you will uncover touch points and obtain knowledge of what the company wants to hear. You will want to integrate into your answers the findings from your research and your understanding of the company operations. Let me give you hypothetical examples of interviewing effectively:

WHY DO YOU WANT TO WORK FOR US?

- Your company has an excellent reputation for providing the best tools and equipment so your team can complete projects on time in a quality-driven environment.

- Your company has strong training and continuing education programs; I continually seek intellectual challenge and thrive in such an environment.

- As I observe your team, I see there is room for advancement. Naturally, I want to master this position. But also, I want to become a valued team player for your company.

- Your company has strong ties to the community, in addition to surpassing performance benchmarks. I want to be a leader in community service as well.

- You have impressed me with your vision for the company, and I want to work with a team that is committed to the highest standards.

- You will see that I have excelled in every position I have held. Your organization has a proven record for developing talent and providing the tools to individuals to expand their skills set while developing new core competencies.

No doubt you will agree that by studying issues in-depth you will be prepared for the complexities of interviewing or a business presentation facing each new business climate. Your list may be different. It really doesn't matter what the question, you must be prepared.

An added benefit to following this method for business presentations is that you will have the tools to win agreements for business proposals. If you will follow this formula for responding to business questions, you will anticipate and overcome objections to business issues and earn credibility. Take time to develop three to six ways to respond to challenging questions. Then you truly will be an asset to your organization.

Now, it is time to send out the résumé. You have rehearsed your answers, but make sure they are not canned responses. Be natural, radiate self-confidence, and use body language to command respect when you walk into the room. You can see all of this in your mind's eye.

Are you prepared for the phone to ring and the telephone-screening interview? Your first hurdle will be the telephone-screening interview. You will want to keep a copy of your résumé and the answers to the questions that you expect nearby for reference. However, what about those questions that you have not anticipated? This is the perfect time to add to your list of potential interview questions. By now, you see interview preparation as an ongoing process. *Practice in front of a mirror*. Rehearse so you can hear yourself delivering the answers that will impress the decision maker and win confidence.

"Do you have any questions?" should be the final question that the interviewer asks at each phase of the interview process. One response can be, "What is the next step?" "Can we make that appointment now?" *Never leave an interview without asking questions. Never!* More importantly, you must ask questions during the entire interview process. Be engaging, show interest and probe to uncover the true issues behind each question.

There are several types of interviews. Sometimes it is an interview with the HR executive or the hiring manager. Other times it is an all-day affair with several executives. Then there is the panel interview. Each takes a different type of preparation.

One of my clients interviewed with Federal Express. He was one of 247 candidates who applied. FedEx selected forty-three candidates to interview at the end of this phase. The recruiter told my client there are forty-three equally qualified candidates. Then FedEx whittled the candidate pool to thirteen. My client had not graduated from high school, but had earned an associate's degree. As delicately as I could, I informed my client that he needed to prepare for the interviewer to call him a "fool" or something worse for not graduating from high school. It was necessary to prepare an answer and deliver it showing superb customer service skills.

When the interviewer pushed him and called him a fool, he said, "Everyone makes mistakes. Companies benefit from their employees who learn from those mistakes. I have learned from mine and I have been an exemplary employee for the last thirteen years. I want to bring that same level of professionalism to the FedEx team." He was hired.

There is the all-day grueling interview with the entire management team. The purpose of this interview is to see if you are a good fit for the organization.

If you are selected for a panel interview, it can be an opportunity to show your presentation skills and distinguish yourself as a leader.

As you ponder the questions that you want to ask the employer, develop a list of questions to ask the interviewer. The materials below provide a list of employers' concerns. You must handle each of the issues before moving the process forward.

WILLIE 
Companies have basic questions you must answer
to their satisfaction:
- Why are you here?
- What can you do for us?
- Can you save us money
- What kind of person are you?
- Will selecting you pose a risk?
- Can we (company) afford you (candidate)?

WILLIE 
Never leave an interview without asking questions!

What questions do you have? Remember the taboos—salary
and benefits.
- What are the skills required to successfully handle the
  position?

- What are your immediate objectives?

- What are your expectations during the first month?
  Quarter? Year?

- Why is this position open?

- When will you make a decision?

- Describe for me the most successful member of your team.

Through a referral, I interviewed with an outplacement firm to handle their small outplacement projects. In the days preceding the meeting, I had sent the material that we used with our résumé and outplacement clients. I met with my contact and we talked for a few minutes. Then she introduced me to the vice president who would make the decision. I coach people on interview preparation frequently, but dancing around in my mind was *how am I going to perform now that I am in the hot seat?*

I had listed the questions that I anticipated. I even developed good answers to each question. The first and only question that fell from the VP's lips was, "What is your passion?" Up until this point in my career, I had never given this question a thought. Passion…passion in my job. I delivered the following answer, "My passion is helping my clients get from where they are to where they want to be…"

After hearing my answer, she stood up, extended her hand, and said, "We'll be doing business." In a few days, I received the commitment letter.

What off-the-wall questions, do you expect? What is your passion?

WILLIE

If you were an animal, which one would you be and why?

How do you eat an Oreo cookie?

WILLIE
Develop a thirty-second commercial about yourself to share with decision makers.

Eight Interview Pointers

1. Prepare a list of questions specific to your job search and prepare for scenario questions. Be prepared for different types of interviews.

2. Develop three to six different answers to each of these questions.

3. Identify the uncomfortable questions that you will be asked, and be prepared.

4. Do as much preparation for the telephone screening interview as you do for the face-to-face ones.

5. Research the company, its vision, mission, and core values. Engage the interviewer and ask questions.

6. Handshakes, posture, eye contact, walking, sitting, and grammar all—give the interviewer a picture of your professionalism—make *presence* work for you.

7. Follow up with a purpose and then follow through.

8. Do everything in your power to make the choice a simple one for the company—become the only candidate they pursue.

Seven Mistakes Job Seekers Can Prevent

You can prevent missteps and mistakes in your job search and career development process by recognizing that companies promote individuals who prepare and execute well. Your job search is one way that you can demonstrate your ability to take care of business.

If you are easily intimidated, the job search process can provide stumbling blocks on your career path. Understanding yourself and the pace that you work is vital. Consider your attitude and listen to the tone of your communication. Even asking a peer or mentor to candidly evaluate your soft skills may give you insight. Make sure you continually make a good impression. Poor communication skills can and will cost you promotions, as will underestimating the need to be punctual, being self-victimized by procrastinating, failing to plan, and providing inaccurate information. These are mistakes that you can prevent and by doing so you will be on your way to connecting more of the job search and career development dots.

1. Thinking You can Wing the Job Search Process

"Good Enough"—If you believe that the way you approach job searching is good enough, you may be right in good times, but when the competition is tight, you may need to rethink your good enough work ethic.

"Good to Great"—To transform a good enough work ethic into a great work ethic you will need to develop goals, create a plan, and execute precisely.

"Give Yourself Permission to Succeed"—If you wing the interview and job search process, what is the likelihood that you will take the initiative and become a top performer. Don't risk a demoralizing outcome! Have a plan and be prepared to succeed.

 **DISSIE**

As an ant, can I wing it?

2. Becoming Intimidated by the Job Search Process

I was having lunch with a friend when she looked down at her plate and said, "I am intimidated by this much food."

The conversation continued with little thought of her statement. A few days later, out of the blue, I recalled her comment. Then I saw the parallel between her words and the job search process. Whether it is building a résumé or preparing for the interview, these challenges unsteady even the most seasoned professional.

"Frequently, I conduct interviews, but this time I'm on the other side of the desk," is what I hear time and gain. Millions of Americans are discouraged, underemployed, and overwhelmed by the process—even more are intimidated by contradictory information. It is imperative that you define a plan and *distinguish between the distractions and real world solutions* that will drive your career forward.

Job searching is like a demanding project that you manage. But this project is a career-long endeavor. It requires preparation, resources, planning, execution, and timely reevaluation. Omitting any of these phases can riddle your plan with mistakes that will lengthen the process.

Contradictions in job search methods muddy the waters. When you put into this murkiness *tips for effective job search* on every career website, you get a soupy pot, which can be toxic to your job search. Many times these tips are mere distractions to your job search plan, which pull you away from your target. By staying on track, connecting the job search dots, and minimizing distractions, you will land a new job.

WILLIE
Ever notice that an ant can follow a trail. I guess they connect dots well.

3. Not Understanding the Importance of Pace in a Job

Companies talk about long sales cycles and one-contact closing, others talk about one-call resolution to customer service issues. There are those whose phone calls are monitored and goals are set to reduce call time from fourteen minutes to eleven minutes with improved results. Some organizations drive product development initiatives in order to launch new products at record speed, while their competitors take longer to capture market share. The pace of the operation can and will impact your job satisfaction.

During the interview process, you want to probe and understand the pace of the company. Is the management team a racehorse, show horse, or workhorse? Many employees are dissatisfied with the pace of their operations. If you are fast and accurate, in some organizations you will be praised, in others you will be told that you are making others on the team look bad.

On several occasions, professionals sit across the desk and I can visibly see their body shake due to the pressure of increasing demands and accelerated requirements. When these same individuals visited other career professionals, they were told, "You need a two-week vacation to decompress before you look for a new job." To prevent job dissatisfaction, understand the pace at which you work, and align yourself with such an organization.

WILLIE 

But don't be afraid to stretch your capabilities.

4. Not Taking Responsibility for Your Attitude

A lady walked into my office and took a seat in the reception area while I was wrapping up with another client. When I was making résumé copies for the first client I said, "I'll be with you in a minute."

"My family and friends say I have a sour attitude. What do you think?"

Stunned, for a few brief seconds, I was without words. We had a fourteen-word exchange and I had no way to measure her attitude, except by the question she asked. I collected my thoughts and said, "What do you think? On a scale of one to ten, with ten being greatest, how would you rate your attitude? Think about it, and we'll talk more about it in a few minutes."

She never answered the question. But when she was seated in my office, she began spewing all the reasons she could not find a job. She had a list of "if I hads" that would make her life better. The "if I hads" were punctuated with the "why I can't." As her story unfolded, she told me about how life was unfair. As gently as I could, I explained that it was necessary that she change her attitude and move on. Employers are not looking for employees with emotional baggage.

Within a few days of the above story, I had another client whose bad attitude preceded him before he walked into my office. This attitude, as I recall, arrived several minutes before he did. I don't know what caused his bad attitude. One observation that I have about attitudes and mindsets is that the root causes are disappointment, envy, or loss. Perhaps it is looking through the lens that "you owe it to me" or "I completed the required steps, but now opportunity is vanishing" or "someone else was given the opportunity, and my skills are better than the person who was hired." Whatever precipitates the bad attitude syndrome, it's your choice on how you respond to disappointment and loss. Unfortunately, if we are honest, most of us at one time or another, have fallen victim to the bad attitude trap. To borrow a sports cliché, "Shake it off and move on!"

 **DISSIE**

But it is my attitude! Can't I keep it?

WILLIE
Only if it is a good attitude!

5. Underestimating the Value of Your Written and Verbal Communication Skill

If you rate your writing and speaking skills below average, you can do something about it. As an English teacher told me, "Writing is not a gift! It is a skill that you can develop." Writing and speaking fall into the same category. They are both talents that improve with regular use.

For two summers, I had the opportunity to spend a few days with high school English teachers as they set the bar for subject mastery. As I listened, I learned English instructors teach to the style book and what they believe to be important. As a writer, the preciseness of the English language is important, but thinking about how to convey a concept is just as valid. Editors are very valuable to the writing process. After writing résumé for clients in all fifty states, nuances in the language change from state to state. As an example, in one state a semicolon helps the flow of content, however, in another state it is never supposed to be used. For better or worse, English teachers are responsible for the writing competency of the state.

English teachers experience challenges in teaching basic language skills based upon learning styles, student attendance, and discipline. For an educated society, communication is vital in interpersonal and business dialogue. Learning the basics of written communication early in one's academic life and then building on that knowledge will provide fundamental skills for promotion.

Compelling and persuasive writing is a valuable skill. To sharpen your written communications *keep a journal* just for you. You will see your skills improve. Continuing education, learning new technologies, and adapting to change is foundational to a solid career plan. Treat yourself to a writing class. Take the time to develop new skills.

You can also enroll in a public speaking class, join Toastmasters International or investigate the Dale Carnegie programs. Practice will improve your skill level. As I listen to good public speakers, I see them continually improve their skills.

 **DISSIE**
I'm a good talker. Why do I need the information?

Next, I want to talk about verbal communication. There are several levels of communication. In a short interview, you have to transition through various levels of communication and build upon each step in the process to earn the confidence of the decision maker or hiring authority.

First, there is the automatic response communication. We learn these responses satisfy most listeners early in our lives. Some people call these clichés.

"How was school today?"

"Fine." (Does anyone really care?)

"How are you?"

"Okay."

"What did you do today?"

"Nothing."

During the interview process, there are also automatic responses as well.

"Did you have any trouble finding us?"

"Not at all."

During the second phase of safe conversation, we communicate indisputable facts moving on to statistical information, measurements, and strategy to be discussed, which lead to the next phase of conversation where a basis for meaningful discussion begins. By engaging in small talk, on some level, a safe conversation ensues, which builds a bridge to the next level of conversation.

"I see that you were a varsity athlete."

"Yes, I played tennis."

"How many members were there in your Marketing Club?"

"There were five officers and twenty-five members."

You will have recruiters ask for an accomplishment-based résumé. Recruiters want the facts and numbers. This is a safe area of communication. While it is difficult for some to talk about their successes, others appear to thrive when talking about their accomplishments.

"Your résumé says that you achieved Rookie of the Year. How did the company recognize you?"

"I won a trip to Las Vegas."

"I see listed in your accomplishments that you added five new customers. What was the financial impact?"

"Those accounts generated $1.5 million annually."

At this phase of the conversation, the interviewer is sending softballs across the net. You can continue in safe mode discussing statistical minutiae, however, the conversation usually turns and you are offered the opportunity to build credibility and trust.

Thirdly, you will find that measurements, statistical data, and strategy can be challenged and debated. Recruiters want to obtain the facts for the emerging decision-making process. This is where diplomacy, tact, and persuasion enter into the realm of conversation. There can be a snare of communication, where a trap is set to attempt to uncover risky information or discredit. Use of hit-and-run tactics or mocking may emerge to make a point. If communication sours and disputes, disgust, or the arrows of *one-upsmanship* are hurled or hinted, you may blow your chance to be hired. As you show respect by listening actively, you may avoid many of the above pitfalls.

"As Rookie of the Year, what were the benchmarks for this award?"

"How many people competed for this award?"

"You said you added five new accounts. Would it have been possible to add more?"

"You said you added $1.5 million in new accounts. Can you verify that?"

"That sounds like a good number, but didn't the Kansas Territory Rookie add $4.1 million in new accounts?"

Finally, when authenticity peeks around the corner, you have the ability to build trust, earn respect, and put leadership capital in your credibility bank. You can show the interviewer you have measurable results and facts along with the ability to diplomatically communicate your perspective in order to drive the agenda forward.

"I am sure that you will agree that building relationships is important. The five new accounts that I developed are now producing $6.9 million in annual revenue. You can see here on the quarterly standings that I continue to outpace my nearest peer.

If you are going to transform the interview into a job offer, you must carefully navigate the interview and not be drawn into a conversational trap. Many companies like to hire safe candidates. Remember to connect the communication dots in your job search by making a credible presentation and avoiding pitfalls.

DISSIE

That is too much information. Yawn! Yawn!

According to Dr. Albert Mehrabian a UCLA Communications Researcher: "7 percent of what we believe is communicated with verbal messages, 38 percent of our vocal message is communicated with tone and pitch, and 55 percent of our communication message is non-verbal."

 **DISSIE**

You mean I need to pay attention to my body language?

Because a friend or family member has read your body language, upon walking into a room, have you heard, "Are you mad?" or "What's wrong with you?" They have just read your non-verbal communication.

WILLIE
Remember to send the interviewer a positive message.

6. While Executing Your Job Search Plan Don't Underestimate Punctuality, Procrastination, Information Tracking, and Planning.

During the job search process, you are building credibility and putting a certain amount of capital in the "hire me" bank.

Punctuality & Time Management: If you need to take a time management course, take one. Master the art of effectiveness and efficiency. You can master your time. To take your career to the next level, you must make the most of your time. I remember talking with an executive about personality tests. "When I take these tests, it always shows that I am not punctual. But I learned early in my career to leave early for meetings in order to avoid being late. It is a practice that I keep to this day."

Many professionals who I know use a list approach to time management. Write down three, ten, twenty-five things that must be done today, and complete them or move them to tomorrow. Franklin Covey, Day-Timer, Microsoft Outlook, and others offer effective time management tools. I am becoming a fan of Microsoft's public and personal calendars along with task tracking. Use what works for you. Your time management tools may change from time-to-time depending on the work environment.

WILLIE 
Procrastination can turn into an Ant Monster!

Procrastination: Many of us fall victim to the procrastination monster. Most of us don't want to return a call where the customer is complaining or worse. If not a customer, it could be a vendor or upper management. Perhaps if we put the project off it will go away.

Rarely does anything go away. If something needs your attention, tackle the project immediately. In my experience, the sooner you defuse an issue, the better the outcome. By responding quickly, taking responsibility, and using a solution-oriented approach, you have the opportunity to become a hero. As a result, you have the opportunity to earn personal capital instead of giving up credibility.

Tracking Information: Systems and processes are very important so you can both follow up and follow through on scheduled phases of projects. Unfortunately, names, phone numbers, and project status will fall through the cracks. Opportunity can be lost along with income. Having a system to track contact appointments and contact information is vital in any effective information management system.

Planning: Regarding planning, I was visiting with a construction project manager and he related to me one of the biggest problems in construction. As I listened to his explanation, he said, "Planning is the key. Too many cost overruns can be attributed to the failure to develop a detailed plan, which can make execution a tangled mess. If the plan is right, deadlines and budget will be met. If not, it is just another project with cost overruns."

It is not just in construction, failing to plan will penetrate all phases of our work life. For many of us, fifteen minutes of planning each day will provide an executable action plan that will show results day in and day out. One professional I know spends fifteen minutes each day planning and produces three times the volume of work as her peers.

After you are hired for a new position, you only have so much professional capital. If you make a misstep and lose some of that capital, it may take months or even years to restore confidence in your ability to perform. Some of the culprits that cause a loss of capital are punctuality, procrastination, your aversion to risk taking and lack of professionalism.

7. Thinking that Goal Setting is Unimportant

It takes goal setting to complete a degree. Unfortunately, I have clients with 150-plus credit hours and no degree. They did not have a goal. It takes goal setting to land a job, unless you are standing on the street and someone walks up to you and says, "Do you want a job?" Stranger things have happened, but it is not likely you will find your next job by just hanging out.

Do not be like one of my friends, who drove the expressway with his résumé in the back seat of his SUV. "Vicki, you said the résumé would work, but no one has stopped and asked for one yet." When he did get around to setting goals and sending them out, he had three callbacks within a few days. Set goals, track your success, and make changes, as the situation requires.

Bonus

Creating or contributing to a toxic work environment can become a mistake in your new position.

I was visiting with a man at a local job fair who wanted a résumé critique. Frankly, I don't remember his résumé, because it was not a résumé issue, it was a behavior issue. He worked in a call center environment and had threatened his supervisor with bodily injury—he was fired. It doesn't matter whether the company created a hostile work environment or the employee retaliated with verbal threats. He had control of his actions, and he made the wrong decision for which there were extreme consequences.

Conflict resolution and anger management can be an issue. If you plan to move your career forward, be the one who finds resolution to workplace complexities. Avoid conflicts of this nature at all costs. Unfortunately, most of us have worked in a toxic environment if only for a brief period. Whether safety regulations are compromised, sales numbers are fudged, or expense accounts are padded, hostile work environments are created or harassment issues raise their ugly head—toxicity contaminates people, processes, and profits.

DISSIE

So, I've caused a few ripples at work!

At the turn of the decade, one of my clients in a multi-unit retail management position who had a record for turning around underperforming stores, called for an update to his résumé. His manager suggested that he skew the numbers on inventory losses to prevent the executive team from terminating him. Knowing that numbers don't lie, he refused to do so. Even with his job in jeopardy, he has core values that ensure the integrity of the numbers for successful decision making.

Recap

On numerous occasions, I have visited with clients in a less than ideal work setting. It could be poor training, bad management, a harassing environment, or other toxic situations that create this milieu. My advice is, "There are good companies out there who are looking for good people, why not find one?" In any toxic environment, you can choose to be a contributor or exclude yourself from harmful conversations or actions.

WILLIE 

Choosing my words carefully and taking responsibility for my actions could build up my professional capital.

Seven Mistakes You Can Prevent

1. Thinking you can "wing it" when looking for a job.

2. Becoming intimidated by the job search process.

3. Not understanding the pace of a new job.

4. Not taking responsibility for your attitude.

5. Relying on less than average communication skills.

6. Underestimating punctuality, procrastination, information tracking and planning during the job search process.

7. Thinking goal setting is unimportant.

Bonus

There are ramifications to creating or contributing to a toxic work environment. Preparation, optimism, job pace, time management, improving communications, effectively tracking information, and setting goals are a few of the job search dots that you must connect to be successful.

Six Career Traps
to Avoid

Several traps can be costly. The first trap is giving up before the job search begins. Then there is becoming close-minded to other opportunities and becoming satisfied with your career. What happens when an employer "Googles" your name? Would it be an embarrassment to the company? Then there is a refusal to relocate and take a promotion. Or you could be trapped in a dead-end job. While these are not all traps for every professional, they have potential to become a distraction, trap, or career killer. Avoid these areas when connecting your job search dots.

1. Believing There Are No Jobs Even When...
   - Unemployment is at 7 percent or 17 percent.
   - There are just no jobs!
   - It's summer time – No one is hiring!
   - No one hires during the Christmas holiday.

It is a fair guess that no one was hiring during Hurricane Katrina, a blizzard, the immediate aftermath of an earthquake, or some other catastrophic event. It is probably more than a fair guess. It is probably a reality, but following an event, as with the build up to special projects, there are jobs.

With any company growth model there are phases to their expansion. Certain project managers, planners, and craftsmen are required at each phase of the project. These jobs may not be the secure jobs of yesterday, but they are the opportunities of today.

Have you noticed that some people are taking advantage of opportunities while others are talking about how bad it is? There are always opportunities. The question is, are you willing to do what it takes to seize the moment?

One professional I know says, "I am too busy solving the problem, while everyone else is still talking about how it can't be done.

WILLIE 
Even in the darkest times, there must be opportunity.

DISSIE

I'll just give up!

2. Not Listening When Someone Wants to Talk With
    You About a New Job

Having a closed mind and not listening to opportunity can be a trap. Listening is not the strength of many people. In fact, not listening is a weakness that we can overcome. Time and again, I hear from an unemployed client, "Recruiters used to call me, but I did not keep up with their contact information." When a recruiter contacts you, even if you're standing in line at a ball game or your phone rings while you're sipping mimosas at the beach, it's smart to listen to what they have to say.

There are many opportunities to sharpen our listening skills, including at home and in the workplace. Perhaps a short-term goal to listen more and longer than normal might pay amazing benefits.

DISSIE

Do I need a file folder?

Do ants have ears?

3.   E-mail Miscommunication, Online Revelations, and Communication Faux Pas

The web offers vast opportunity and career traps as well. You can use the information obtained through internet research to streamline many of your assigned tasks. It also has traps. And not using it wisely can be damaging to your career and credibility. Some companies perform data mining to see if their employees are actively involved in a job search. Many employers check your Facebook page to learn about your habits.

Communicating electronically is a time saver. It is ideal for quick questions and transferring information. This can be a trap if used unwisely prior to getting a new job along with a big mistake after landing your new position.

Resist the urge to tell a recruiter how you feel about his or her lack of communication. Recently, I read a posting about a career article online. Job seekers were spewing venom and venting their frustrations. After reading a few of the comments, I decided 90 percent of the people with an opinion would not make a good employee at this point-in-time. Use your writing skills to make a positive contribution.

But when it comes to criticism or negative feedback, it can have a mushroom effect, when simple issues are blown out of proportion because of poorly selected words or the perceived tone of the e-mail. Unfortunately, you have little control of perceptions.

Bonus

Before you send your first e-mail to secure your next job, you need to analyze your e-mail address. Is it professional? Some e-mail addresses that can trigger a negative reaction:

- Gonefishing@aol.com

- Golfing@aol.com

- LazyC@hotmail.com

- Skydiving4fun@gmail.com

1. Respond promptly to e-mail messages.
2. Reject profane, rude, arrogant, sarcastic, and obnoxious language.
3. Reread your correspondence, use spell check and grammar check before sending the message.
4. Reply, but don't use the CC and BCC too frequently.
5. Re-examine your subject line—does it tell the recipient about the content?

6. Ramble not—use clear, concise, compelling language.

7. Rushing is not appropriate in dealing with e-mails—you may send the wrong message

DISSIE

Surely, my employer will not mind if I apply to one job today. They'd never fire me for this, would they?

4. By Not Evaluating a Career Move to a New Location, You Could Find Yourself in a Trap

Relocation cuts both ways—it can be a trap or the best opportunity ever. With any product life cycle, jobs are created, moved, and eliminated, most in the name of resource management. Regional industrial centers for specific products transition to new geographic locations. Global economy, support services, manufacturing, and customer service, among others, have transitioned to sites worldwide. Tribes of technical professionals along with their families are migrating domestically and globally to secure lucrative job opportunities.

Nomadic lifestyle has become the norm in many industries. I have written résumés for general managers of major retail chains whose career spans ten GM positions in ten different cities over a ten-year period. The military is known for relocating frequently, as is corporate America.

One of my clients who wanted to teach English in Korea was extolling the virtues of living in South Korea and working for a language school. He had traveled to Korea and was enamored with his experience. When I met him he asked me to draft a résumé for his dream job. Later he shared with me that his dream job became a nightmare of poor living conditions and a nonexistent paycheck. He found himself writing home for the money to get a plane ticket so he could move back to the United States. The last time we visited he was happy to back in the United States.

There have been times when I received international calls from my clients or a referral where the caller needs a résumé for a contract job. It could be in security, oil field construction, pipe line operations, or support industries requiring purchasing, inspection and quality control expertise.

Relocating brings with it many of the blessings and curses of a nomadic lifestyle. Saying yes may offer a career growth or a lateral move, but saying no could bring a career plateau.

5. Being Trapped in a Dead- End Job

If you are working too many hours to look for a job, there is not room for career growth with your current employer, or you're working in a toxic work environment, it is time to step outside your comfort zone and pursue other interests. Sometimes this may be easier said than done, because you are at the top of your pay grade and you will need to prepare for a salary adjustment to make a change. This may require a plan and a scheduled exit.

Toxicity in the work place emerges in various forms. It can be a bad boss with unrealistic expectations, belittlement, badgering, micromanaging, sexual harassment or intimidation or all of the above. When you are in a job where your values conflict with those of the organization, it can damage your reputation or health if you don't handle the stress and pressure. I have visited with professionals who will do anything to get out of the immediate situation.

There was one client who came into my office shaking from the pressure and stress. She had witnessed a twenty-eight-year old coworker pass out at work from the strain. One employee left a baby in a hot car and the baby died. This company was the poster for "pressure cooker". It was also listed as one of the best places to work in the area and made national publications for their record of success. For some employees it was the best job they had ever had, for others it devastated their lives.

Employees become trapped or charmed by their income, because it is above industry standard. Success in its early stages is like a hypnotic trance. The money is flowing and little thought is given to the consequences of long hours, under appreciation and loss of family time. By the time there is a moral breakdown, ethical compromise, family breakup, health issue or personal breakdown, toxicity has permeated the employee's life.

One of my clients was a successful manager for a fast food restaurant and had a heart attack. After his health was restored, he went into construction in order to find a job with less pressure.

I was talking with a nurse manager, who was working too many hours. She said, "There is no one to take care of my clients but me. They will fall through the cracks if I don't take care of them." I suggested a shorter work week and to find a way to alleviate her stress.

If you are an hourly worker, you may find a better job with less stress and better pay, but you will need to diligently search for such a position.

One day I was talking with a single mom who was working smart. She sold wireless phones and services. She also sold real estate and one business fed the other. Over the years she had maintained the same cell phone number. She is a smart marketer.

Several women have sat across the desk from me telling the story of sexual harassment. Improper behavior of managers is in every profession. When an employee gets a hint of such behavior, get out of the situation as quickly as possible. There is nothing but grief to follow. Good companies do not tolerate such behavior from their managers.

I have another client who was a manager for a national retail chain. She had a medical problem due to a work related injury. Pressure soon followed and she exited the company, but not before taking the *Financial Peace* course and getting her financial affairs in order. She had a year's income saved.

If you are single you can usually handle the long hours. But as family responsibilities make their way to your plate, it become more difficult to juggle all of the family dinners, family visits, time with friends and special interests. When your identity is tied to your job, it is a challenge to separate them. It is a hard lesson, but you are not your job and your job is not you.

If you want to know how I know this, I am prone to be a workaholic. Take it from me—there is more to life than work.

When you are trapped in a dead-end job, create a plan and work your plan.

Remember it is always easier finding a job when you have a job.

6. Targeting Jobs above Your Experience Level, Impatience Regarding Promotion, Upwardly Mobile Career Track and Career Transitions

While we live in a culture of instant gratification, some skills are learned gradually over time. I remember interviewing a boat pilot who worked on the Mississippi River. He told me it takes years of apprenticeship before a pilot earns the distinction of captain. There are numerous underwater hazards and it takes experience to fully understand the danger of a misguided action. Learning, observation, listening, and patience are all catalyst in becoming an executive leader.

There are many positions where you can achieve rapid promotions. The ceiling is usually low in these organizations. Once you achieve a certain level, the lucrative position can turn into a dead-end trap. *Something can be said for appreciating your current situation.*

At first blush, this client appears to be dissatisfied with his career growth. He updated his résumé every ninety days. While there was turmoil in his industry, he had a good job. Every quarter he would apply for positions with other industry leaders. I remember asking, "My résumés are working for my clients and they are landing interviews, is yours working for you?"

"Yes, I have had several interviews. I have been testing the market to see if I am employable and that my skills are in demand. My current employer is taking good care of me. I am fortunate. I just want to be prepared if something changes."

If you are with a good company, be appreciative of your opportunities. Take advantage of learning as much as you can and broadening your skills. If you need more training to get a promotion, take the initiative, and get more training.

Sometimes we only recognize the gift of unemployment in the rear view mirror of life. An executive sold his business and was somewhat dismayed that he was not getting any traction in his job search. It was late May, he sold his business in February and no one was interested. I told him to be patient and something would work out. In late summer, he stopped by again. There was some interest beginning to percolate. "Now I see what you meant when you told me to be patient. I really did not know my ten-year-old son. We got acquainted this summer. This has been the best summer of my life and it has been good for him too. We are Buds."

Six Career Traps

1. Believing there are no jobs in any economy.
2. Not listening when someone wants to talk to you about a new opportunity.
3. E-mail miscommunications, online revelations, and faux pas.
4. Not evaluating a career move to a new location.
5. Not recognizing you are trapped in a dead-end job.
6. Impatience regarding promotions and an upward mobility career track—not appreciating your current job situation.

Recognizing the reality of the job market, listening, observing, patience, an open mind toward relocations, and shaking loose from a dead-end job are among a few more of the dots that you must connect.

Hey guys don't make a misstep, watch out for the traps.

Five Old-School Job Search Techniques That Still Work Today

1. Research and Read Newspapers, Industry Publications and Business Journals

Get current job leads downloaded to your phone. Tap into LinkedIn or Facebook for job leads or purchase Job's subscription services, because you know information is the key as you approach your job search. Identify the companies that are in a growth pattern with unblocked potential. By reading newspapers and industry publications along with scanning electronic journals and resources, you will be able to determine the latest trends in your industry. You may even get a tip about how to and who to approach with companies.

A library card can get you access to databases and complex marketing research. You may end up with information overload; however, a trip to a major library can produce benefits now and in your future job. Both reading newspapers and using your library card are old-school concepts that still work today. The added benefit of independent research is that you obtain thought-provoking concepts that prevent you from becoming too comfortable with your knowledge base. Getting comfortable can put a drag on your career and income level.

DISSIE

Why can't I wing it?

2. Using Your Newly Found Time to Volunteer

Most job search experts agree that using your time wisely by volunteering can be an asset to your next career move. You could target organizations that have meaning to you. Or you could focus on an organization that your targeted employer is supporting with their time and money. Either way you will find it rewarding to give back and help others. You may find your passion for living outside of yourself and continue your service after you find your next job.

From time to time, I volunteer and consult with non-profits helping the underserved in our communities find jobs and resources.

I am known for exaggerating to make a point. One day at a networking breakfast, where I volunteer with the

Hospitality Committee for the Metro Chamber of Commerce, it was my turn to introduce my business and I said something like, "I can help anyone find a job if they will listen to me, execute a job search plan, show up, and become a good employee." A year or so later the president with a non-profit organization contacted me and reminded me of my quote. She went on to tell me that she worked with individuals released from prison, recovering from disabilities, and others facing challenges in finding a job in today's workplace.

"Could you come to my office and consult with my counselors? You said you could help *anyone?*" We agreed on a time and place. After I hung up the phone, I thought to myself, "What in the world are you going to tell these counselors. You've put yourself in a box this time."

I have a tool that you will find in the fourth chapter. By customizing this tool, the counselors were able to list the obstacles to finding work and potential employers for their clients while at the same time using their creativity to list potential job avenues for their clients.

In the note that I received from the president a few weeks later she said, "We use the tool you designed for us every day and we are placing more of our clients."

On another occasion, I was asked to speak to a group of women served by the Salvation Army and offer advice on job search. I asked, "Tell me about something good in your life." One of the participants responded, "There has been nothing good in my life—ever."

Others in the group agreed. If someone had kicked me, it would not have had a more profound impact. I continued to probe in order to get the group to think about something good they had experienced. "Here is a piece of paper, I want you to write down something good that has happened to you."

After a few minutes, her eyes brightened and she said, "I can remember something now." However, she was uncomfortable sharing the information with the group. Others in the group reached back in their memory and found good stories to write down on their sheet of paper. I asked them to carry the story in their pocket and read it every day until something good happened to them again.

If you are struggling with discouragement, why not write down your successes and read them every day until you can add to your story. You will find this to be a very rewarding exercise. Go back to the end of the third chapter and write your success story.

Perhaps you will find volunteering as rewarding as I do. You can make a significant contribution, because there is such a great need.

1. Dress, Determination, and Diligence Have Value

Could you imagine being passed over for a job because you asked the question, "Do you allow casual attire at work?" By using your observation skills, you can determine appropriate dress requirements. Successful candidates for employment have discipline and know the value of punctuality, regular attendance, and tenacity. After doing your homework and investigating companies, you will be armed with the knowledge to make a good first impression. In most instances, the first impression is the only one that counts.

DISSIE

Why do I need to worry about my dress? I'm comfortable and that is all that matters.

I was visiting with a client who was seeking an international position. He asked, "How do I dress for the interview?" Knowing that most global employers are more formal than we are in Middle America, I said, "Do you know anyone employed with a global company that has offices in the area who regularly travels internationally for business? If you do know someone, ask them the question; if not, research the company's executives online and observe their dress." Always dress for the job you want, not the job you have. My advice is to look crisp and polished in either business or casual attire. Remember the "little things" like a good hair cut, polished shoes, brushed teeth, mouthwash, makeup (for women), flattering professional outfit.

DISSIE

If I can do the job, what is the big fuss?

4. Networking and Developing Business Contacts

One of my executive clients had negotiated a merger and he found himself unemployed. He dropped by my office between his office and home on his last day on the job. "It is finished and I need to find a job. Do I need to find a recruiter? Or job readiness professional?"

I said, "Those are a couple of ways to find a job, but don't you have a little black book with your business contacts? If I were in your shoes, I'd go home and begin dialing all of my contacts. Someone in your address books is bound to know someone looking for a leader with your expertise."

About thirty days later, the executive's wife dropped by to say she was selling the house and moving to the East Coast where her husband had landed his new job.

Today we would use LinkedIn, Outlook or our cell phone directories to make those contacts, but the principle is the same.

DISSIE

The only time I touch base with my network is when I need something.

WILLIE

Maybe you need to give a little before you asked for something.

5. Printed Presentation of Your Résumé and Cover Letters

With all the electronic applications, no one needs a printed résumé and cover letter. Everything is paperless—everything. Or is it? Printed résumés are a necessity today.

Time and again, I asked the question, "What key is your finger on when you read your e-mails?" Most of the time my finger is on the "Delete" key. It doesn't matter whether I delete the file or not, I am mentally erasing the information. While it is generational, many decision makers still want to read information on a piece of paper. You may find it to your advantage to print your résumé and present it to an employer. That same generation will ask you to e-mail your résumé.

When you want to move your résumé from the "black hole" in a database, you may need to give the decision maker a nudge and provide them with information so they can find you quickly. Well-written letters can make a difference in landing lucrative positions. As you build your templates for your job search, you will need a cover letter, a follow-up letter (where the company has not responded), a broadcast letter to blanket decision makers, and a "thank you for the interview" letter. When it comes down to two equally qualified candidates, the one sending the thank you letter will land the job almost every time.

WILLIE 
Don't you like to be appreciated?

Developing a Solid Work Record: When I first met R.O., she was a successful sales representative for a large overnight delivery company. She excelled and ranked in the top five percent among her peers. She went on to relocate and manage the federal account for a large imaging company. While in this role she earned an MBA and ranking in the top six percent when ranked with her peers. R.O. wanted to reach new career heights and obtain a position in medical sales. She applied to a company that wanted a candidate with only two employers and record of accomplishment academically and professionally. They recruited top 10 percenters. And she landed the position. More and more I am hearing that employers want to hire people with a good work record that spans three years or more in longevity.

Five Old-School Job Search Concepts That Still Work Today

1. Research and read industry publications, newspapers, and business journals.

2. Use your newly found time to volunteer.

3. Dress appropriately, express your determination, and show your diligence.

4. Network to develop business contacts.

5. Use paper copies of your résumé and cover letter.

Develop a solid work record. Other job search dots that you must connect are the need to keep abreast of industry trends, give back to the community as a volunteer, dress appropriately, show your determination, optimize your network, and develop a solid work record.

Four Career Killers

1. Dishonesty

At this point, I could stand on the proverbial soapbox and extol the virtues of honesty. Perhaps I could throw in a few platitudes or quotes from leaders and philosophers. Suffice to say, choices are around every corner. Seemingly, many are inconsequential, or are they?

Corporate executives fall into the trap of misstating their credentials on their résumé. Some claim to have degrees they didn't earn. This killer mistake is not only in the executive suite. According to research, more than 50 percent of applicants stretch the truth on their résumé. It has been called "Resumegate"—poor judgment, dishonesty, etc. But it is not just the executive floor; it is rampant throughout many corporations.

Some corporate leaders have resigned under fire, others have been dismissed, and others forfeited bonuses and other incentives. There are those who skate by with no visible repercussions. I am sure you would agree there is a loss of credibility.

Companies and agencies audit employment applications. I was asked to write a letter requesting reinstatement following the termination of an employee from a federal agency. This individual had completed two years of studies at a community college, but didn't attend graduation or even follow up to obtain his degree. During an audit, it was determined that he was six hours short of an associate degree. He was dismissed. In order to unravel the mess, he went back to the community college to research the problem. He discovered that he was six hours short, and he asked them what he could do to obtain an associate's degree. At that point, they told him they would award the six hours and the degree based on his work experience. I wrote the letter explaining the circumstances and asking for reinstatement.

It can be very damaging to your career and pocketbook to misstate career information on your résumé. If a specific degree, certification, or license is required to be successful in your field, commit the time to obtain these necessary credentials.

I wrote a résumé for a client who was proud of winning a Harley for his over-the-top performance. He had transitioned to another industry and was ready to pursue new interests again. Initially, he did not receive his résumé copies. One day while I was working on an update for one of my clients, who was sitting across the desk from me, the client who won the Harley dropped by and sat quietly in our reception area.

While visiting with the client needing an update, spontaneously he began to tell me the story of how he had almost won a Harley. A few days after the corporate competition ended and the Harley was awarded, at the close of the shift, the winning manager was making change out of the cash register without ringing up the sales. Unfortunately for him, an executive from a competitive organization stopped by to pick up a call-in order. When this executive observed the procedures, he called the owner and the general manager was fired. The client of several years said, "I'd love to meet up with the scoundrel." We concluded our business and my client left. I went to greet my waiting client. He was nowhere to be found. This was an intriguing coincidence at best.

On another occasion, a department manager was fired because he would *not* skew some financial numbers. He was worried and rightfully so. It can be tricky dealing with questions regarding a termination. Many of my clients have wrinkles in their past that must be written around. This was just one of those situations. On his résumé, we stressed the value of providing a set of integrity-based financial records. The first company that he approached was seeking such a professional. He found a new job quickly.

Once more, I received a call from one of my clients needing a résumé update. As we talked, about the new turns in his career, he said, "We need to remove bachelor's degree, because I did not complete degree requirements." I would like to tell you that this has happened only once, but I can't do that. Are our sensibilities so dulled by corporate indiscretions that we have come to expect dishonesty?

2. Discrimination

Discrimination intrudes in the workplace, taking many forms. Gender, health, weight, religion, and race are among the many areas of discriminatory actions. You may have experienced other discriminatory acts in the workplace. Whether it is reducing the labor force by eliminating positions of diabetics, individuals with disabilities, or cancer survivors—discrimination is one of the labels that could apply. When corporate policy or the decision making of department heads rollout practices for the greater good or in the name of profit, discrimination may be lurking in the corner.

How does this information impact job searching? While it may not impact you, unless you are unemployed, discrimination impacts many job seekers. Can you lift fifty pounds or read eight-point type without corrective lenses? Early in my career, women were beginning to make inroads into the workplace. I remember being told by a client that he did not believe that I could write his résumé because I was a woman. If there is a way to neutralize preconceptions and prejudices, I have not found it. What I have discovered is that if you are a content expert, you will earn respect. More often than not, through diplomacy you will distinguish yourself as the go-to person.

Frequently, I tell my staff, "You can't argue with a fool." If someone's attitudes and beliefs are written in stone, I will not change their perspective, even with strong evidence. This is one of the "Vickisms" that we repeat often in our office.

Another "Vickism" is "You can't fix stupid." Stupid is perhaps too strong. However, when someone will not consider a different viewpoint, they are not using their full mental capacity nor critical thinking skills. While I cannot take original authorship to either of the "Vickisms", I use them occasionally when someone is slow on the uptake, where evidence contradicts preconceived notions.

When it comes to discrimination, nothing good can come from bias in the workplace. However, no topic is more polarizing than discrimination and racism specifically. At the urging of my clients and friends, I want to discuss the whale in the swimming pool and give the topic some ink.

My career has been shaped by writings of Viktor Frankl. After spending time in the German concentration camp, he concluded there are two types of people in the world—the decent and the indecent. You may want to read his book, *Man's Search for Meaning.* There are many types of discrimination, and from my perspective, discrimination crosses social, economic, and racial boundaries. I have interviewed thousands of people and we all bring our biases and prejudices into the culture.

To put further perspective to my opinions on this matter, I was raised in a small community, which was very ethnically mixed. There were immigrants from Eastern and Western Europe, Hispanics, Native Americans, and African Americans. The area was and is heavily influenced by Baptist and Catholic traditions. Fifty years later, I see changes in the culture when parishioners speak with reverence and appreciation for their priests from different ethnic backgrounds.

Unfortunately, disrespect crosses the time continuums and cultural differences. In retrospect, I am not sure that attitudes of the past are anything more than the conflict of decent and indecent people walking through life. Even walking through life today, we see the drama of discrimination played out. We also see the theatrical performance with false accusations.

Any hint of racism or discrimination, and we see the daily drama of personal destruction, demonization, divisiveness, and the drive to silence critics play out on the national stage.

Perhaps we need a way to shine a light on bad actions in an effort to offer hope and redemption. Too bad we can't have a funeral and bury the words and actions of racism, bigotry, and discrimination. Then bring to life, respect, and appreciation for various cultures.

Discrimination is subtle. It is hidden from view of polite society. One of my clients, a successful educator and administrator, works with inner city students. She has a reputation for giving more of herself and her time on projects that nurture and challenge students. Her passion for educating is reflected in the success of her students. While she is not alone, she has a reputation for challenging teachers to excel. As an administrator, she identified the issues as a blame game. "The teachers blame the parents, the parents blame the teachers, and our students get short-changed. As the principal, I can't get the teachers to accept responsibility for serving our communities and providing more than classroom instruction. They don't want to do any more than what is necessary to get a paycheck. Something is lost in today's professionalism."

While this sounds harsh, it does give us a window into the culture of education from her perspective. I want to add here that she is one of the best educators that I have met. She has a daughter in corporate America who has a seat at the decision-making table. She has taught her children to do their best and not to expect special treatment because of race. This has served her family well. When meeting this role model, you never see color—you see her personality and professionalism.

This educator has found her passion and strives to erase color from her corner of the world. Her story is an inspiration to any educator striving to make a difference while challenging our children to succeed.

If you are asking why this information is in a book about connecting the job search dots, it is because I see diversity impacting the workplace. Also, you may be facing this environment. Some want to ignore the topic, but ignoring it does not make it go away.

Since we are discussing educators, here is another story. I was talking with another educator who works with at-risk students in a rural school. His students can't make it in a regular classroom. He told me, "Going back three generations, no one in these students' families has graduated from high school. I find it very rewarding when I can encourage students to hang in there and graduate."

Early in my career, I was a regional director for Professional Résumé and Writing Service. I supervised as many as sixteen offices in six states. I remember two clients who needed résumés in Montgomery, Alabama. Both of these clients had degrees from the same university with the same numbers of years of experience. One was a state senator's son who was earning a mid-eighties salary. The other was an African American woman making less than $30,000 annually.

While there have been many similar stories, these are the ones that hold a place in the gray matter of my brain. One of my expatriate clients put discrimination into focus for me. He said, "I work with an international team of executives. Each nationality has a way of doing business." He went through each nationality and gave me the corresponding differentiating trait, and then he said, "They call me *the Cowboy.*"

Differentiating between characteristics and discrimination are two totally different matters. As long as we fall in the category of being a decent individual, everyone wins. Remember respect along with appreciation for another perspective can and will build bridges in the workplace.

Over the years, I have heard stories of bad behavior on behalf of managers, who created a hostile work environment, made unwanted sexual advances, and have not made an offer based upon religion or race. Then there is unspoken practice of "I will not hire you if you smoke." "I will not hire you if you are overweight." "You can't be on my team if you're a member of a specific religious group." "If you have a serious medical condition, there is not a place for you in the organization." And the list goes on. We would all be well served if we treat others as we want to be treated. What a novel ideal, I wonder who said this first.

As I visit with clients, I use the following example: if I were being interviewed by a company with an ethnic workforce, I doubt that I would be hired. The same could be said for being interviewed by an under thirty-year-old management team. I am not sure it is appropriate to label either of these examples as discriminatory behavior. With any scenarios, there are exceptions and caveats.

A very attractive African American professional shared with me her thoughts of the difficulty in interviewing with a white recruiter. She did not share the following information until she felt it safe to do so. She expressed how difficult it was to respond to interview questions. She felt her answers needed to be run through a black/white filter. She was somewhat stunned when she was selected for the position. Many times perceptions are totally invalid by both the interviewee and the interviewer.

WILLIE
At all cost, avoid stereotyping and stereotypical behavior.

3. Discontentment Is Definitely a Career Killer.

I have attended numerous workshops where the presenter talks about the "5 percenters." These people are the ones who consistently find something wrong with everything. They stir the proverbial pot and keep the office or workplace in turmoil. Many times, they are angry, unhappy, contentious, and their actions are toxic and they poison projects.

I was visiting with a gentleman who couldn't understand why he could not find a job. He had been dismissed for creating a hostile work environment, not to mention the legal liability for his employer. If you need conflict resolution or diversity training, you might want to consider such training.

There was another client who completed a degree and was bitter because she could not get a position in her chosen field. She spewed toxicity in almost every word of her conversations. She was very unpleasant to be around. Employers were silent after she submitted her résumé.

The only one who can change your way of thinking is you. Shift your mental gear and find an area where you reinforce positive, hope-filled and confident possibilities. Reliving all the negative things that intrude on your life will become a negative drain on your potential.

WILLIE 
Contentment comes from within. Slow down long enough so contentment can catch up with you.

4. Distractions

Distractions! We all have them in our lives, and from time to time it is difficult to distinguish between the noise and the issues at hand. When our team members are engulfed with distractions, it has the potential to paralyze the entire team.

Identifying presenting problems and differentiating between those issues and the defining problems that are at hand can be a challenge. Whether it is unemployment and you need a job, or it is a special project with the team, peel away the clutter and find the root problem so it can be solved. You will find examples of my observations listed below.

Frequently, I hear, "I can do anything." And when I do, I want the client to define anything. A narrow definition is looming. In this example, it is necessary to help the client find focus. Reality dictates that anything is not anything with a job, career, or calling. Here, I peel away clutter and help the client find focus.

Repeatedly, I hear, "I want a normal job with regular hours. Also, I want a matching 401K, health insurance, and great pay." These jobs are available with many companies. Most of the time, this client is looking for security.

Commonly, I hear from an under-qualified client, "I want a management position." In this example, what is management? Is it managing people? Is it managing resources? What areas of management and operations are of most interest? In this arena, we need to educate the client about the sequence of career steps. Rarely do under-qualified candidates get a management position. And when they do, that is another topic for discussion. What do you want to accomplish?

About 15 percent of our clients would rather tinker with the résumé than approach the turbulent job market. Call it fear of the unknown, intimidation of the process, or perfection gone wild. Anything that keeps you from fast-tracking your job search is a distraction. Transform those distractions into a plan that will overcome obstacles.

WILLIE

There are consequences to dishonesty, discrimination, discontentment, and to allowing distraction to intrude on your work life.

WILLIE
Perspective! Ethical behavior and honesty should be expected, as should acceptance, respect, a can-do attitude, and the ability to identify root causes of business issues.

Three Job Search Wishes

After interviewing clients for over twenty years, I have noticed that some deal with "if only I hads" while others have career wishes. If I only had time to pursue an education, I could…. If only I had the money to pay back my student loans… If I had a better boss, I could get a promotion… If I had better transportation, I could…and the list goes on.

If you had three job search wishes, what would they be? For a few brief minutes, we are going to deal in the fantasy realm. A handful of my clients would rather deal in the areas of wishes rather than in the area of reality.

One day, I was dealing with a rather pragmatic client who desired a career change and had visited with career counselors but could not get any direction to a career change. What do you want to do? This question falls from my lips hundreds of times each year. After several "I don't knows," and more and more probing he said, "I like board games and spending time with my children."

"Have you contacted the major toy company to see if they need a sales representative?"

"But they wouldn't hire me, would they?"

"You will not know if you are a candidate for such a position until you pursue your options."

He had the skills, education, and knowledge-base to contact major buyers, conduct executive-level presentations, and close sales.

On another occasion, I had a client who wanted to become a futurist. Not knowing exactly what he meant by the title futurist, I asked, "What are the skills required to becoming a futurist?"

"Math and science."

"Do you have those skills?"

"No."

"I am not good in math and science, but I want to be a futurist."

Most of the time we need to identify our strengths and map out strategies to find a better job. You will be more successful if you deal with the realities of the job search.

Now back to you. Make a list of your three career wishes.

____

____

____

You will find listed below some of what I commonly hear.

- **Would you wish for more money?** Many of my clients would wish for more money. You may be one of those who want more money. You can find a better job, sell your assets, get a performance-based raise, win the lottery, marry well, inherit millions from a rich uncle, win a sweepstake, win an accident or disability claim, or take up stealing as a career. If you had more money, what would you do with it?

- **Would you wish for a lifestyle without work?** Every now and then, I talk with someone who says, "I don't want to work." You may need to find a rich spouse. Here again you could bet on sports, visit the casinos to gamble, get lucky, become ill with a debilitating illness, get convicted of a crime, win a product liability lawsuit, become homeless. Work might be the best alternative.

- **Would you wish for more time?** There are days that I wish for more time. With more time, there is both a blessing and a curse. It could be more time to produce, more time to worry, more time for leisure. Thankfully, time is standard for each of us.

This is a good place to deal with fantasies that could sideline your career. What are the dragons that keep you from focusing on your future?

____

____

____

Two Plans to
Take You to the Top :
Life Plan/Career
Disaster Plan

In MBA programs throughout the country, SWOT (strengths, weaknesses, opportunities and threats) analyses are the outline for creating a strategic plan that will illuminate uncharted business terrain. Perhaps you have created one or many SWOT analyses outlining the *strengths* of the program, *weakness* in the process, *opportunities* that emerge from the horizon, and *threats* that could sink your program. The SWOT assessment offers the opportunity to take a 360 degree view of your projects and layout the details so you will be successful in your endeavor.

Nothing, absolutely nothing, takes the place of preparedness. A career plan is essential in taking your career to the next level. With the right plan, you will avoid the career pitfalls that plague your peers. I was discussing career options with a manufacturing professional and he said, "It is all about the plan. If the plan is right, the system implementation and deployment will have minimum setbacks. If the plan is flawed there are problems—many times big ones!"

There are two plans essential to your career. First, begin with a life and career plan. Where do you want to be as a person five years from today? What are your career goals for the next one, two, three, four, and five years? Do you have educational goals? Have you identified a mentor to help you navigate the turbulent waters of an upwardly mobile career? You will need an accountability partner to help you track your benchmarks.

In your life and career plan, you will need to identify financial goals, health, and fitness objectives; a continued education process; a legacy, volunteer, and philanthropic plans to support worthwhile endeavors, you will even need a leisure plan. And let's not forget the retirement plan to build and protect wealth. You may have a list of what you want to accomplish before you're thirty-five, fifty-five, seventy-five, and one hundred five. If you don't, you may want to develop one.

Perhaps the most important plan for your future is a disaster plan. Before you dismiss this, as that will never happen to me, let's recall some of the disasters of the past ten years. When I initially wrote this, Hurricane Katrina was fresh in my memory. I was having a quiet evening with my daughter in Dallas when she received a call informing her that approximately 1,000 residents of New Orleans were on buses and would be arriving in the suburb where she lived.

"They need our help! Let's go," my daugher said. As I looked in the faces of the displaced residents of New Orleans, I realized this could happen to any of us.

In 2010, there was the environmental blow to the Gulf States from oil spewing into the water after an oilrig explosion. With the total environmental impact unknown, the rate of job loss was devastating.

More recently, our hearts broke for the victims of the Japan earthquake, tsunami, and nuclear leak crisis, as it does for the tornado victims of Joplin, Tuscaloosa, and other parts of the country. These acts of nature and weather-related events bring destruction in a matter of minutes. In recent years, we have experienced ice storms that took out our electrical infrastructure, which took weeks to restore. Jobs were lost and income evaporated. Companies closed their doors.

The Oklahoma City Bombing and even September 11, 2001, brought a significant blow to our state's economy along with personal loss, national sadness, and vulnerability.

Whether it is the death of a close family member, key member of the management team of your company, or a significant downturn in the economy, we are susceptible to calamity. It could be earthquakes, fires, weather disasters, financial missteps, or even corruption. You must be prepared to reshape your career, if you find yourself a victim of an event outside of your control.

WILLIE 
Taking a few minutes to create a "what-if plan" that you hope you never need, could prove beneficial should you need it.

Planning and preparation are two of the *big dots* that you must connect in your career.

You're the One!

You have within your grasp the means to make life-changing decisions that will take your career to the next level. Most of us have read biographies of Colonel Sanders of the KFC fame and J.C. Penney, the retail chain founder. In each decade, there are leaders who overcome obstacles and achieve great things. Many technology industry leaders of today have bounced back from adversity. Countless stories are yet to be written. And if you haven't read these stories or other similar ones, you may want to add a biography to your reading list.

Few things are more inspirational than reading stories about regular people who do extraordinary things. The next story written could be about you. Why not? Every week I hear stories from my clients about overcoming barriers and navigating detours in their careers.

One of my clients sat down and told me his story. There had been a significant downturn in the energy industry. "You see I didn't graduate from high school and I only made $80,000 last year. Do you think that I am doing a good job supporting my family?"

I am sure the words, "Of course!" flew out of my mouth

like a bullet. The response was automatic. He had made the decision to explore new career options and needed a résumé that told his story effectively.

What made this story so memorable was the very next client who walked into the office said, "I have an MBA and earned $25,000 last year. Do you think that I am doing okay?" I responded, "It sounds like you need a better résumé to tell your story so you can increase your income."

You may need more education, a life coach, or the self-motivation to create and execute a self-marketing plan to take your career to the next level. I am sure you will agree that settling for mediocrity is not your best option. Where do you want to be one year from today—personally and professionally? As you look down your road to the next decade, where do you want to be in five years? In ten years?

Sitting across the desk from me several years ago was a professional in his mid-fifties. To begin the conversation, he said, "I got my high school sweetheart pregnant and I have worked hard to get where I am today. For our product, I am the number-one sales representative in the nation. It has taken a lot of hard work. I have succeeded where others have failed." I am sure you will agree this statement falls into the category of "too much information."

He lived in a sparsely populated state with miles of cornfields between each town. He had to drive many miles each year to deliver success for his company and his clients.

Another client told me that she spent seven years completing her education and seven years refining her professional skills. The next seven years were spent in administration leading teams. When I met her, she was taking the next step and advancing her career even higher.

I have interviewed thousands of professionals and craftsmen seeking new job opportunities. During this time, I have provided direction to others seeking a first start or a new start in establishing careers. Some want to use their transferrable skills to find new employment and reinvent themselves. Many times, I hear stories of success. Other times I hear about failure. And there are the times that I get more information than I need to write a résumé and cover letter.

When you are telling your story, it is not necessary to provide the details of a divorce, character failures, or other personal information. Employers are not hiring you for your failures or your shortcomings. They are hiring you because of your strengths.

Some failures will preclude you from obtaining employment in certain industries, but not all. While there are times, I need details. Many times, it is just unnecessary information.

When your identity is wrapped in your job, you need to redefine yourself and realize that you are you. You are not the *job*. It is the healthy thing to do.

WILLIE

There is a good job out there for you! It may take time, education, training, and determination. But you can do it!

Are you ready to connect your specific job search dots?

Zero—
What's in a Zero?

Nothing one might say. Zilch would ring in the ears of some. A zero with the rim rubbed out would appear in the mind's eye of others. Perhaps an empty glass or container would flash before your eyes. Zero is nothing—or is it?

- Zero interest persuades some to purchase big-ticket items while striking fear in the hearts of individuals earning interest on investments.

- For one generation it is the number they used to make a collect telephone call or obtain information from a telephone operator, but for another it means the name of a rock band.

- Zero calories excite dieters or the health conscious while going unnoticed by others.

- Ground Zero incites an array of emotions from devastation to anger and on to hope.

- Zero customers would strike fear in any businessperson while adding a zero to the current number of accounts would most likely add to the bottom line.

- Zero defects or delinquencies would inspire ongoing excellence.

- Zero to three in child development is where the foundation for lifelong learning begins. Could it be said that on any new job the learning curve is zero to three years, before your career advances to the next level?

- Zero inflation is sometimes good and not so good.

- Paying zero for high-dollar health benefits as an employee incentive is very enticing.

- Zero score at athletic events disappoints, unless there are already numbers on the scoreboard.

- Zero on the thermostat is chilling.

- Zero stress might be the envy of some, while others thrive on the adrenaline rush.

After examining zero and the nothingness of the numeric number, what would it require of you to add one zero to your income? Would it require more education? Would it require better tools? Would it require a different outlook? Would it require more discipline? Or would it require better preparation?

You must ask one question of yourself. "Is adding a *zero* worth the price?" Sometimes *zero* is more than nothing! In reality, examining *zero* could be the flashpoint required to take your career to the next level, but that is up to you, isn't it? *Zero* can be nothing or by adding a *zero*, your income may exceed your wildest dream.

Why not make it a goal to add $5,000 or $10,000 dollars to your income. You may want to set a goal of adding a zero to your income within the next five years. To borrow words of wisdom, "When you aim for the moon, if you miss it—you'll land among the stars."

WILLIE

If I had zero crumbs that would be awful—I would not have anything to do! But if I added a zero to the number of crumbs I carry each day, that would astound the other ants and put me on the path to greatness!

A Few Final Words

While this book is not all about money and how money equals success, it is about living up to your potential and making all you can, so you can save all you can and then give all you can. Money, salary, and return on investment are among the dots that you must connect as you pursue your career. Most of us work for a paycheck and not out of the goodness of our hearts. A reasonable compensation is expected.

Many of us find a job that we love and stay with it during the ups and downs of business cycles. Others transition from career to career trying to find their niche. Some find the job they love evaporating before their eyes. Unfortunately, we can't change reality, but can find a career in the new economy—whatever it may be.

By building a plan and executing that plan, we can prevent career stagnation and accelerate career growth. Through goal setting, we can continually improve our skills and strive to take our career to the next level.

If we get caught up in fantasy careers and wishes, or fall prey to career killers, traps, mistakes, and missteps, we may sabotage the career of our dream.

As we leverage old school concepts along with tried and true methods for landing a new job, interviewing effectively, and taking advantage of opportunity, we improve our odds in the ultimate job hunt.

As the interview process takes on new life, by adapting to not only the questions, but communication styles and tactics, we compete on the race track for success. Résumé development will evolve as well. Jargon will emerge as new skill sets are required to master emerging technologies.

Finally, make a friend with technological innovations. The number of professionals using smart phones is creeping up daily as they perform job searches, communicate online, send pictures, and talk with family and friends. No one knows what innovations tomorrow will bring, but don't be afraid of newness—embrace technology.

What is stopping you? It is time to connect your job search dots for success.

APPENDIX

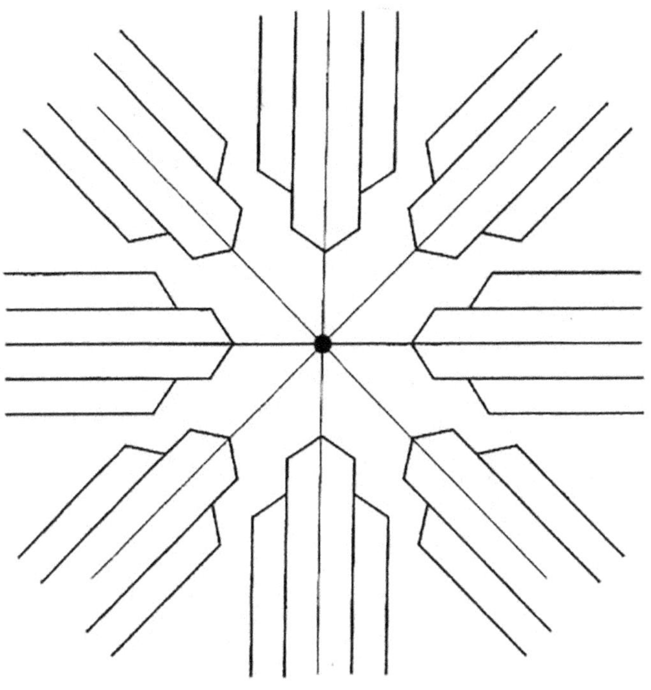